BETWEEN THE TUMOR AND THE TOMB

A Diary of Doom and Deliverance

*Yea, though I walk through the
valley of the shadow of death...*

by
Kim Manning Nguyen

TABLE OF CONTENTS

FOREWORD
BY DR. SCOTT SHAPIRO

"The following book by Kim Nguyen demonstrates that she is a woman who is never at a loss for words. Kim is a devoted wife and mother, is very religious and is determined to survive. That is demonstrated nicely in this heartfelt book. It is always a devastating moment when a human being learns that they have a primary brain tumor. However, all hope is not lost and Kim gives a good emotional account of the highs and lows of dealing with a primary brain tumor. Kim is alive, beautiful and energetic and this story is very real and compelling.

I have devoted my life to operating on human brain tumors. I am not sure if being Lance Armstrong's brain surgeon was a blessing or a curse. Now, everyone that comes to me with a brain tumor thinks they will get the same result. Despite successful surgery the tumor can return and shorten the life span of patients. It is very gratifying when patients succeed and live a long, productive life and it is heart wrenching when all treatments that we as doctors try do not succeed in curing the patient. It is my wish that Kim will live a long, long time, but there are no guarantees in life. That makes this book all the more compelling."

Dr. Scott Shapiro, neurosurgeon

CHAPTER | 1

I Have a Headache!

It is one doozey of a headache which starts it all! It is June 4, 2003. This in itself should be my red flag. For, you see, God created me to rarely have headaches. I rarely need Tylenol. This day I do.

JUNE 3, 2003

My family and I are planning to take a 14-hour drive to Florida for a vacation, leaving on June 4th. But on June 3rd at 10:00 p.m. it is my loving, caring, adorable husband, Tom, who asks me, "Hon, do you have everything ready for you and the kids?"

"Wow," I think, "How in the world could I forget to pack?" I reply, "No, Hon."

He responds, "I guess we're not going to Florida in the morning." Well, he is right.

I ask if we can still go somewhere close by such as Chicago. We really need to get away as a family and enjoy each other. Life does tend to get stressful and we all need this vacation. He says, "That's fine with me."

It is late evening when I go to the computer to do a search for the lodging. My brother Steve just happens to work in the hotel business and as a result we are very fortunate to get great rates. For some reason, I feel led to book the Four Points in Chicago.

Packing for a family of six is quite an undertaking. Tom finishes packing. I get their favorite clothing together and into the suitcases which Tom loads into the van. Now we go to sleep so we can start fresh in the morning. Chicago is much closer to Indianapolis than Florida is.

June 4, 2003

I awake this morning and my head is just pounding away. Is it from the stress of forgetting about the trip? Can it just be all the hurrying and change of vacation plans that is causing it? Needless to say, I tell Tom: "Hon, I really have this terrible headache." I think to myself, "I can't remember when I have ever had a headache, but I know I've never had one this bad."

Tom tells me "Hon, let's not go to Chicago. We should stay home because you're not going to have a good time. I'd rather you get some good rest."

I say, "No, it's okay. I know it's only going to get better because it surely isn't going to get any worse!"

We leave Indy and head north to Chicago. But, during the three-plus hours it takes us to drive, my headaches just don't seem to want to go away; they are getting worse! I am actually to the point where I begin to massage my upper right gums with my Oral B spinning toothbrush which I just purchased.

Well, Tom sees this, and hears it as well, since I am sitting on the passenger side of the van. He says, "Hon, let's head back home; you're feeling miserable."

I say, "No, it'll be fine, really!" I know in my mind we just need to get away and have a short vacation with the kids because family time is extremely important. Everyone has always told me to enjoy the kids while they are young because those years just fly by. They are all getting older and "everyone" is so right.

We finally arrive at the hotel. We check in and get the luggage up to our room. The pivoting moment in my life's journey is just as it says in Jeremiah 33:3. In just a moment you will understand why this verse is most significant to me!

Of course, right off the bat, Calvin (10), Collin (8), Rachel (5 ½) and Spencer (2 ½) years old want to go to the pool and swim. We get our swimsuits on and head to the indoor pool. I sit at the white table in the pool area while Tom takes the kids into the pool. Tom is such a wonderful husband and father. The kids are on him like honey on a comb. Their laughter echoes throughout the entire pool area. I am enjoying just watching them have a fun time. They are jumping from the side of the pool right into daddy's arms. They are all having a ball.

I continue to have this headache, though. I start rubbing my right temple. It seems as though all the pain is located there so I think I can massage it away. The hot-tub is near and begins to look enticing. Well, I do have my swimsuit on so I take the liberty to go into it. My thought is the hot-tub certainly looks as though it will somehow relax me enough to get the ache out of my brain. I sit on the bench deep beneath the bubbling water. The sound is so soothing; I believe this will work. I give it about 30 minutes and then I realize it does help a little, but the reality is I am just wrinkling up.

I meander back to my chair near the kids and continue to rub my temple. As I sit there I single out a lady who is helping a young, mentally-handicapped lady get into the hot tub. For some reason I feel a strong urge to talk with her. She surely resembles our dear friend Marcia whom we call "Mom Jorg." I get up again and head back to that hot tub. I begin a conversation with the two. I'm actually just like my dad when it comes to talking, since he and I tend to have a "knack" for speaking with people.

I begin by saying, "Excuse me, my name is Kim and I wonder if you may know of any remedies to help with headaches? I really have a bad one!"

She replies, "Hi, my name is Ruth and this is my daughter Lisa Joy. If my other daughter were here, she'd know exactly what to do because she gets really bad migraines. Honey, you might call 1-800-Migraine if there's such a number. I'm sorry I can't be of better help."

I say, "Thank you Ruth!" My thoughts are, "How will I ever get any relief from this?!"

About five minutes pass and our daughter Rachel yells from the pool, "Mommy, I need to go to the restroom!" As all parents know, with or without a headache, it's a responsibility 24/7 and it's one that I wouldn't trade for absolutely anything! So, I get up and walk with her. As we proceed through the doors, Ruth and Lisa Joy do, too.

My new friend says, "Kim, I have another number for you, honey."

I say, "What's that, Ruth?"

"It's Jeremiah 33:3. It's in the Bible. Do you read it?"

I reply, "Yes, Ruth, I am a Christian. I really don't read it as I should, but yes, I know."

She replies, "It says, *'Call to me and I will answer you and tell you great and unsearchable things you do not know.'*"

I reply, "Ruth, thank you. That is all I've been doing: praying and asking God to help me."

She says, "Oh, honey, I know you have. Sometimes we just don't understand *why* we have to go through tough times. And in your situation, you may be wondering why God isn't taking all this pain away. I mean, we know He is God!"

I said, "Yes, I agree with you."

She replies, "Kim, just keep praying. Prayer works."

I reply, "I will!" What Ruth doesn't know is that lately my spiritual life has been stagnant. That's part of why I wanted to go on this vacation. I think that we just need it as a family and maybe God could show me how to have more joy. My Bible is on a shelf and I have not been reading it lately nor can I recite verses as Ruth does. I see she has a good trait and I think it would be a great help if I knew more Scripture verses like she does.

After a couple hours, the kids are finally ready to get out of the pool and are getting hungry. They are all shivering until I give them warm and, most importantly, dry towels. As we begin to head to the door, Ruth comes to me and says, "Kim, you and Tom have a beautiful family. I'm thinking that if you continue to have this headache, you might want to think seriously about going to the hospital while you are here in Chicago. Honey, headaches can be a sign of other health problems."

I reply, "Ruth, you really think so?"

She says, "Yes. In fact, I really think you need to have a complete check up once you get back home."

"I will, Ruth. Thank you for your concern." I then boldly utter, "Ruth, I need to ask you something. Why are you here at this hotel this weekend?"

Her response surprises me. She says, "My husband and I are missionaries and we are here for a seminar this weekend. We just have a break in our day and Lisa Joy wanted to swim. She's on the Special Olympics swim team."

Ruth could have literally knocked me over with a Tonka truck! "Wow," I think to myself, "God works with total strangers who just happen to be here at the same time and place. I could have chosen any hotel but this is where we are to vacation. If we would have stuck with our original plans we might have been in Florida today and we would not ever have met Ruth and Lisa Joy. This is wild! Is meeting her just a coincidence?" I boldly ask Ruth for her phone number before we leave the pool so I can keep in touch. She gives it to me.

Side note here: I will misplace her number over time but when I am cleaning I shall stumble upon a notebook where I will find the piece of loose paper with her number written on it and I will call her. Just as I would still have the loose piece of paper I wrote Dr. Meng's number on. It truly amazes me that I never lost those two loose pieces of paper.

I did call Ruth and she was very surprised, yet happy to hear from me. She told me she and Lisa Joy had wondered how my health was. She assured me that they had always kept me in their prayers and asked God to help with me with my headache and my health. Boy was she ever amazed at the story I had to tell of the journey! Remember, it was out of boldness I had asked her for her phone number. But as you can see, it was all for a reason. She was ecstatic to hear I was doing well. I'm grateful that she was able to reap a blessing of knowing that God used her to help me, a total stranger, a year or so before, in order to find out about the headache! This continues to amaze me!

Now, back to Chicago. We go to our room to get ready for the next adventure. The kids love all the excitement of being in a different place and the fact that they get to go swimming in a pool. Tom is aware that the headache isn't leaving and I'm just not feeling like my old self. He gets on the phone and calls our niece, Elizabeth, who lives here and is a medical student studying to become a physician. He asks for her thoughts. She strongly suggests a specific over-the-counter medication.

Before he hangs up he asks her where her favorite Vietnamese restaurant is and asks if he can pick her up to come see me. She agrees and they meet at her apartment which isn't far from the hotel. He stops and gets the medication and they head back. I take the medicine as soon as they arrive. Elizabeth says that it may take a couple hours to kick in.

But, in the meantime, the kids are antsy and hungry. We are dressing and getting ready to go to this highly favorable restaurant.

I'm just hoping the medication kicks in. Being out with family like this does help take my mind off the headache. Mom has always said something like: "it's mind over matter. Don't focus on the problem; it may only get worse. Think about pleasant things." The wise anti-dotes which she has given me over the years, are now coming to mind and really do work. Mom is so wise!

It is just a headache and pretty soon the medicine will kick in and it will go away. Right now I'm thinking I'm on a beach in Hawaii! What a nice thought!

I am so caught up in the hour of visiting and eating some delicious food that my focus is on the visit and not the pain. Afterwards, we have a difficult time finding parking near Elizabeth's apartment, but we manage. She invites us up to see her place and to meet her roommate, another female medical student. Wow, what a beautiful apartment they have! Its balcony has such a stunning view of the city. We sit and talk about life and she is so amazed at how fast the kids are growing. We are, too. She asks, "How's the medicine working?"

I tell her, "I feel much better, thank you. It's actually bearable now."

She echoes Ruth's advice by saying, "If it doesn't get better, go see your doctor!" I thank Elizabeth for her knowledge.

We ask her if she'd like to go with us the next day to the Shedd Aquarium but she has to study, plus she was just there earlier this week. We understand and tell her it is so nice that we were able to visit with her. She tells us about some other events going on in the city that the kids might like to go to. We really are having a great time here and I'm certain I will continue to feel better.

CHAPTER | 2

Found Nemo and I'm Dori

JUNE 5, 2003

I wake up feeling much better this morning. I really don't think I will have to seek medical care while we're here. That medicine did work better than I thought. The kids want to go to Shedd Aquarium today. It is an annual trip we make and they really enjoy seeing all the different types of fish. I'm feeling up to going now and Tom says then we will go. The kids are so excited!

Tom is really good with the streets here. His memory is so sharp with directions. He even remembers where the area in Chicago known as Vietnamese Town is. This is the area in which we will eat more Vietnamese food later. I don't remember the area, but I'm so glad he does because it's a great neighborhood with lots of authentic Vietnamese favorites of our family.

We arrive at Shedd Aquarium and the kids are so ready to have this adventure for the day. Actually, I am too. When we are in the Coral Reef section, Spencer says "Daddy, look, there's Nemo!" Nemo is a talking orange-and-white clown fish in the movie entitled "Finding Nemo." It is fresh on his mind since we had seen it recently.

Tom and I laugh and Tom says, "Yeah, you are right Spencer. You have a good memory!"

I can so relate to the "Dori" character. Her role is played by a fish that has a bad memory of almost everything. I had a lot of "duhs" recently. It's ironic because I even referred to myself as Dori the day of the movie because *I think* I am having some short-term memory problems. I have always had the best memory of all my siblings.

We are now wrapping up our time here and the kids want to go swimming back at the hotel one more time before we head for home. The headache isn't the way it was at the beginning of the trip. It's getting better, *I think*?! At some point I will get it looked at by a doctor. But, really I'm having a great time with the kids and Tom on this vacation! I'm looking at the bright side of this situation.

CHAPTER | 3

Promise Kept

JUNE 9, 2003

When we get home I actually call my doctor since I'm still taking pain meds for the headache. I think it must be something to do with a tooth. Maybe it is the upper right crown that's causing this?! I call my dentist's office and speak with Jean. She schedules an appointment with Dr. Rosenfeld. I'm just certain that when he takes an x-ray of it, he will have the answer to what's the matter with me! He happens to have an available appointment that day so I tell Tom and add, "I think it's ok for me to drive since he's only 20 minutes away! Besides, I have my cell phone and will call you if I have any problems getting there."

He says, "Ok, if you think you're okay to drive, I'll stay home with the kids."

Before I leave the house I take some more pain pills, the same ones I've been taking. During the drive it is kind of strange, because I take a wrong turn. *Ok, why did I just do that? I am so forgetful lately. I mean I've been to this office so many times and now I turn at the wrong stop light. I even burned the spaghetti when I forgot it was on the stove cooking for dinner the other night. I have a lot of forgetfulness lately for some reason!*

19

Finally I arrive and I'm even on time in spite of the mini detour. Dr. Rosenfeld greets me with his beautiful smile and then has me sit in the dental chair so he can take a look at what may be causing the problem. I describe to him the pain over the weekend and tell him I'm so glad he is able to see me on such short notice. He says, "Kim, let me take a look at it. Actually, Kim, it looks fine." He proceeds to take an x-ray of the upper right crown area and discovers a tiny cavity next to the crown. He doesn't think the crown or cavity has anything to do with the headache, but says he will fill it.

As he shoots my gum with the Novocaine; it literally feels as if fire shoots up the entire right side of my face. My tear duct suddenly shoots out tears. *"What is going on?!"* I say to Dr. Rosenfeld, "That just felt like liquid fire. Is this normal?"

He emphatically says, "No, Kim it's *not* normal. You might want to get checked out by your family physician and get to the root of this headache and I'll fill the cavity later. It could be a migraine or yet another health issue."

Sounding familiar? Chicago's Ruth has said the same. What he doesn't know is I don't have a primary care physician.

After I leave, I call Tom and tell him everything is ok with the crown. "I am heading home." The pain medicine is helping so I *think* maybe things will be fine.

CHAPTER | 4

Do I Have to Hit You in the Head to Get Your ATTENTION?!

JUNE 24, 2003

It is now two weeks later, and I'm still doing fine with the over-the-counter headache medicine. But, now a turn of events gets things going! **Sometimes it takes something drastic for us to re-examine our situation and raise red flags.** *This day's events allowed that to happen; I'm so thankful and you will now see why. Things happen for a reason even when we don't understand that reason.*

A couple of weeks have gone by after my dental visit and it is a day I will not ever forget! It is Rachel's sixth birthday. She says she wants it to be a girls'-only day. But I take Spencer since he wants to play, as well as five of her friends, to the local putt-putt golf course. I do this even though I continue to have the headache. I find it's *manageable* with the pain pills.

We are having a great time and Rachel absolutely loves the "girl's night out" with her friends. When we are about halfway finished Spencer informs me that he needs to go to the bathroom. Well, what am I to do? I quickly think to ask Jennica, who is a six-grader that Rachel invited to this party, if she can take over until I get him to the potty. She says, "No problem." So, I gently place my yellow golf ball into her hand and thank her.

Because of the extent of his potty time I see the girls are now almost finished with the course. As we are walking back I spot Jennica and shout, "Thank you so much for helping out with the girls!"

She replies, "No problem. Oh yeah, Kim, here's your ball." She then tosses it up and I go to catch it from a short distance but it seems to be moving in slow motion or something. I fail to catch it and it actually ends up hitting my head. She runs up to me and says, "I'm so sorry! Does it hurt?!"

I tell her, "Yes, it hurts really badly but don't worry about it. I think it's time for us to go home now." She agrees. She begins to gather up all the clubs and the balls and returns them to the office. I stand in the parking lot and rub my right temple. I actually say a prayer in my mind: "Lord, why did that golf ball have to hit me right where the headache is?"

I hear in a clear conscious thought: "In a couple of days you will get some news and you'll not have the headache any longer."

I wonder to myself, "What in the world does this mean?!"

Jennica now has the kids and meets me and is still feeling so bad. I tell her not to worry about it and I even thank her for being such a great help with the girls. I tell her I really don't know what I would have done without her! We head back home to have the party's grand finale. On the way home I call Tom and tell him of the events and he can't believe it!

Fortunately, it's only a seven-minute drive. I'm thinking as I drive, "This is really a strange thing to happen with that golf ball." We arrive and Tom is waiting at the door to console me. He tells me to go lie down and he will take over until the party ends. I go brush my teeth and rest my head for the night. I'm thankful that Rachel didn't have a sleepover birthday party. She had wanted one, but we thought maybe next year when she is seven. Another "God thing," as you will see presently.

CHAPTER | 5

The Reason!

JUNE 25, 2003

It is 5:20 a.m. as I wake up. The alarm doesn't ring; it's the headache that wakes me, this time in the manner of an alarm clock. It's ringing loud and clear; red flags are flying high. I sit up and hold my head and tell Tom my head hurts "really-really badly." It feels as though it is going to burst open, not a pretty thought. Tom is consoling me once again and asking what can he do to help. I don't know what to tell him because if he really knew how bad it feels he might think I'm at death's door. Am I? I have never before felt this much pain.

The first thing I can think of is to call my Ob/Gyn, Dr. Hua Meng. He is the doctor who delivered our four children. I remember that he gave me a private line to call at the hospital if I had any concerns. But that was 11 years ago. I tell Tom, "There is one thing you can do."

He says, "You name it!"

I tell him, "I feel I should call Dr. Meng. His number is on the inside of the cabinet door above the kitchen phone on a piece of notebook paper." He rushes to get it and I walk to the dining room to meet him. As he hands it to me, I just fall to the floor. I'm not hurt and tell him, "Dial the number for me, please!" He does, and to my surprise, Dr. Meng answers!

I say, "Dr. Meng, this is Kim Nguyen. Did the call transfer to your home?

"No, I'm on call. What's the problem?" I tell him about the headache and yesterdays' golf ball incident and how I just awakened to the **horrendous** headache!

He replies, "Kim, I'm the opposite-end doctor but I will help you! You may be having a stroke. Do you have any way of checking your blood pressure?"

*As God and Tom are my witnesses, I look to the right of my foot where I sit and I spot something. To my amazement, there is a blood pressure kit. It belonged to my father-in-law, Phat Van Nguyen, who passed away a mere five months earlier. I had been saving it for my parents, but I'm glad I procrastinated getting it to them. **This is really wild!*** I tell him, "Yes, I have one here next to my right foot and I will ask Tom to check my pressure. I relay the numbers to him.

He replies, "Kim, you're not having a stroke! But something is going on and since this isn't my line of expertise I want you to call the Medical Diagnosis Center here at the hospital; they can help you." He then proceeds to give me the number and says, "Give them a call at eight when they open."

"Dr. Meng, thank you for helping and caring for me!"

He humbly replies, "Kim, I just want to help you feel better. It's my job."

We spend the next 2 ½ hours trying to figure out what is going on. I only know that for my entire life until now I've not had any headaches like this one. I take more medicine to help numb the pain. *I'm surely glad that golf ball hit me because maybe it was the Lord's way of getting my attention?!*

It's now eight o'clock sharp and I phone them. A pleasant-sounding voice greets me. I say, "Good morning. I have just spoken with my doctor and he wants me to be seen by the first available physician."

She says, "We have nine specialists, which does he want you to be seen by?"

I say again to her, "the first available one."

She says, "What do you need to been seen for?"

I tell her, "My guess is to rule out migraines because I'm having headaches and the one this morning woke me up."

She replies, "I'm not a nurse, so I'm not sure which one will be the one that needs to see you. So, call your doctor back and ask him."

"Ok, I will. Thank you," I say. I hang up so fast and call Dr. Meng. His nurse Sylvia answers. She tells me she will ask him and then will call me right back.

This is the account from Nurse Sylvia of what happens next: Dr. Meng calls MDC and speaks with an internist. That physician says to him, "She really needs to be seen by Neurology. In order for her to be seen would you feel comfortable ordering a head CT for your OB patient?" He says yes to the CT order.

Sylvia calls me back and says Dr. Meng is ordering a head CT and also wants to check for the flushed feeling which I'm having as well. She says something about having my blood drawn to rule out hypoglycemia. She proceeds to tell me the appointment times for the CT and then the blood draw. I thank her for helping me. She gives me comforting words before we end our discussion.

I tell Tom about the appointments. He and I are thankful I'm going to be checked out. It has taken a while but I will actually get the check up that Ruth has told me to get! *I am thankful for that golf ball incident! I guess it must have happened for a reason.*

CHAPTER | 6

*First CT of My Life:
Diagnosis Please!*

JUNE 26, 2003

CT: a method of examining body organs by scanning them with X rays and using a computer to construct a series of cross-sectional scans along a single axis [syn: computerized tomography, computed tomography, CT, computerized axial tomography, computed axial tomography, CAT]

Hypoglycemia (n): abnormally low blood sugar usually resulting from excessive insulin or a poor diet [syn: hypoglycemia] [ant: hyperglycemia]

Source: *WordNet ® 2.0, © University*

Just as planned I am now getting ready for my CT scan this morning. Something is strange though. I don't have any more headaches. Well, thinking back to the golf ball incident it has now been two days since it hit. And I recall the insight I believe the Lord gave me about "not going to have any headaches in a couple days." This is strange but true. I get ready and Tom does, too.

Tom and I are a little bit anxious, but not too much because we assume it has to be something to do with migraines. The forgetfulness that I'm experiencing can happen to anyone. I really don't know what to think about the flushed feeling but that's why I'm getting that blood work. Everything will be just fine, I'm sure of it!

Tom drives us to Indiana University Medical Center; we park and go to the registration desk of the hospital to check in. According to the clerk, there aren't any orders yet for the scan. *What do you bet that when someone originally saw the CT order written by an OB/Gyn Physician, he or she may have thought it was a mistake?* These are just my thoughts. This little bump in the road doesn't stop me because I'm a very determined person; it's how I was created! I look at this as a challenge because I am on a mission to get ***something*** accomplished today and I will!

Next we head to the second floor of the hospital and go to the Coleman Center because I know they will be able to retrieve the indispensable orders to have this head scan performed today! This is where my OB/Gyn, Dr. Meng's office is. It isn't open yet but I know someone will be in very soon so we wait about five minutes until one of the office staff comes in. I explain to her the brief version of *why* I am asking for the order from Dr. Meng for this CT. I know he ordered the tests and his nurse Sylvia took care of it.

The receptionist searches to find the order but isn't successful… until nurse Patrina walks past. She knows me and about this out-of-the-ordinary scan for which there is definitely an order. Coincidently, she also tells me she is the one who originally faxed it. She knows exactly where to find the original order; she makes another copy and hands it to me. This is definitely not a coincidence!

We now head back downstairs to hand it to the same hospital registration desk clerk and she says, "That was fast."

30

I tell her, "I know the right people."

Tom says something like, "So that's why it always takes you a long time at your appointments. You do a lot of visiting!"

I tell him, "Yes, I know a lot of folks here, and you know me and how I love to talk." Tom and I smile at each other.

*See, this is just how the Lord created and wired me: bold and determined. Otherwise, we could have left and headed back home and waited for the X-ray department scheduler to call us and say they finally had the orders from my doctor. But, no, not Kim "Possible" Nguyen. I'm on this mission to get **something** accomplished today and I do it with determination. I'm thankful for how He wired me 30+ years ago!*

We now head to the basement where the scan is to be performed. We meet the loveliest receptionist in the MRI Department; her name is Audrey. What a beautiful smile she has! She is a positive and upbeat person and I'm glad about that. She hands me a clip board after I hand her the order along with my registration paper. She instructs me to fill out the front and back sides of the questionnaire.

A few minutes pass, then I hear my name and I head to the scan. Tom is told to remain in the waiting area.

Side note: Since I'm now a regular, routine patient, I'm well known around that hospital. Not only am I known as a patient but also as one who enjoys making cookies. I make special cookie deliveries for my doctors, nurses and techs as well as the receptionists I've grown to know. We are like one big family here. One time a nurse passed by me and said, "Do you work here? I see you all of the time around the hospital."

I told her, "No, I'm just a former brain tumor patient here for my routine scans and appointments." I'm delighted with all my new friends here at Indiana Medical Center and the Indiana Cancer Center. They are hopeful for the best with my health! They are all wonderful to be around!

I head to the CT machine. It reminds me of a big donut, and I'm the filling. The nurse starts asking questions and I answer. She explains what they are going to be doing with this scan, and about the fear that is often associated with going into a closed unit: I may experience claustrophobia, she says. Since I've never been in this situation before, I am about to find out if I have this phobia, and I hope they will discover whatever else is going on.

The nurse explains the feeling I will have when they inject my veins with the "contrast dye." She tells me, "Don't be alarmed when the dye goes in. It may feel as though you wet your pants." But she assures me that's the way it should feel.

She then says, "Do you have any questions?"

I say "Are you going to find out if I have migraines with this test?"

She glances at me with a most bewildered look and says, "Honey, this test isn't used to find migraines."

I reply, "Then why are you doing it?"

She responds, "***To rule out mass***."

As I sit and ponder her words I think to myself; "Mass, mass of what?" I then say, "What do you mean by ruling out mass?

Looking stunned, she replies, "To rule out TUMORS." When she says "tumors" it echoes in my head much like a shout in a tunnel. And the words echo. It is very much like that.

I reply, "There are no tumors in there. Go ahead and do your test!"

As I lie calmly on the gurney at the entrance to this machine, I have such a peace. Despite what was just said to me, I am able to be at peace. I think, "This is just the standard procedure that they must do." In my thoughts are all our family and friends praying for the Lord's will to be done with my situation. They and we know that God is in complete control of the outcome of this sophisticated test. The tech administering the test is probably thinking I have no clue how serious this can turn out to be. This is so true!

After the procedure, I throw my legs over to the right of the gurney and tell her, "You are so right about that feeling of wetting my pants. I didn't, did I?"

She smiles and says, "No." I stand up but I feel a little bit dizzy. She tells me to sit until the feeling passes.

After about three minutes I stand and begin to leave the room. I'm thinking to myself, "The nurses and techs now have the information that my doctor needs." I ask them for the results but they say a doctor needs to look the x-rays over first. I then say to the male tech, "I'm now heading to have some blood work done. They are checking to see if I'm hypoglycemic. Do you think the results will be available before I leave today?

He replies, "What time is your appointment?"

"Nine o'clock."

33

He says, while stroking my right forearm, "Yes, I think you'll know something by then." I thank him and off we go to get the lab work done now. *Boy, we surely are getting a lot of exercise with all this walking!*

CHAPTER | 7

Now Checking for Hypoglycemia

We arrive early for my appointment. I sign in at the second front desk of my morning rounds at the hospital. *My! Making rounds; I'm not even a doctor or nurse!* I check in and then sit and read the magazines. Tom and I talk some but it seems as though it's just another routine doctor visit. The last time Tom was with me in this very waiting room was when we were pregnant with Spencer. Oh, I'm definitely not pregnant. We even joke about if I were.

After about ten minutes, Dr. Meng's Nurse, Sylvia, comes out into the waiting area. She says, "Hi Kim, Dr. Meng is on the phone for you."

I reply, "Hi Sylvia. I just had that head CT performed; do you think they have the results, yet?"

Because of my detailed mind, I notice that her pattern is similar to that of the tech who had sent me from the x-ray department. He had rubbed my right forearm and she did as well.

As she rubs my arm she says, "Yes, Kim, I think he knows something."

I think to myself, "Everyone is in such a good mood with all this rubbing of my arm stuff." There surely are a lot of "duhs" going on with me. I really am like that fish named Dori from the movie "Finding Nemo" that I mentioned earlier. She had lots of "duh" moments and forgetfulness just as I do.

CHAPTER 8

It's Not Good News!

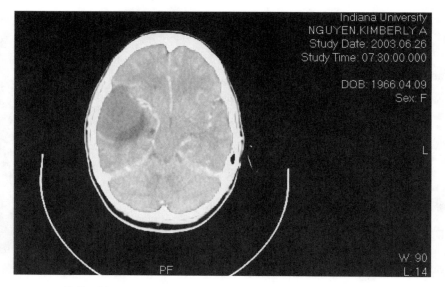

MY RADIOLOGY CONSULTATION REPORT

"Exam Date: 06/26/2003, Exam Time: 07:58AM

*Impression: Large right middle cranial fossa mass with mild vasogenic edema as well as subfalcine and uncal herniation. No intracranial hemorrhage. Differential diagnosis would include low-grade astrocytoma, ganglioglioma or oligodendroglioma. Findings were discussed with the **ordering physician** shortly upon completion of the examination."*

Sylvia and Nurse Cindy lead me to Dr. Meng's office and he is waiting on the other end of the phone. They stay with me and I sit at the desk. I say with a cheerful voice, "Hi Dr. Meng! Do you know the results from my test?"

He says, "Hi Kim. Yes, that's why I'm calling. I'm sorry I can't be there in person but I'm at Wishard Hospital. Sylvia and Cindy are in with you, correct?"

"Yes!"

"Ok, good. The news isn't good, though."

My now cheerful voice is panic-stricken and I feel my heart pound hard. "What do you mean?" I say.

He replies, "Kim, you have a brain tumor. They tell me it's quite large and that they think it's cancer!"

I say, "Dr. Meng, you have to be kidding?!"

He says, "I really wish I was, but, it's true. Kim, this is quite a serious matter. Is Tom with you?"

"Yes, but he's in the waiting area." He then tells me I need to tell him.

I said, "You really think so?"

He emphatically says, "Yes!"

*It's another "duh" to be experienced in my journey. A **TUMOR**: Wow, how can this be? Just an hour ago the CT tech was doing the test to rule it out! I guess one really is in there?!*

Dr. Meng tells me that Tom and I should stay put at Coleman because Sylvia has arranged for a team of neurologist interns to do some neurological tests and also for a neurosurgeon, Dr. Scott Shapiro, to explain what the next plan of action should be. I thank him!

Sylvia says, "Are you ok?"

"I'll be just fine!" She, Cindy and I all hug. I have a plaque at home that says, "Nurses are God's angels on earth." I truly think angels are placed in my path today. They bring comfort.

Only a few minutes pass by, but I gather the strength needed to walk out of the room to my next consultation room. Sylvia and Cindy go to Tom in the waiting area and direct him to where I am.

As I'm walking out of the room, Nurse Linda walks with me in the hallway and says, "Kim, you look like a zombie."

I tell her, "It's unbelievable news. It just can't be! I have a brain tumor and they think it could be cancer!"

She comforts me too and says, "Just know you and your family are in our prayers." I thank her and we hug.

I'm literally walking through that valley.

*Even though I walk through the **valley** of the **shadow** of death, [Or through the darkest **valley**] I will fear no evil, for you are with me; your rod and your staff, they comfort me.*
(Psalm 23:4)

Surreal 1: marked by the intense irrational reality of a dream; *also*: **UNBELIEVABLE, FANTASTIC** <*surreal* sums of money> source: *Merriam Webster Dictionary*

Real: 2 a: not artificial, fraudulent, or illusory: **GENUINE** <*real* gold>; *also*: being precisely what the name implies <a *real* professional> b (1): occurring or existing in actuality

I'm now at the appointed room and I sit motionless until Tom arrives. By the look on his face I can see he is concerned. I tell him about the tumor and about the interns and the neurosurgeon who are on their way to discuss it all with us. He and I hug and he rubs my back to comfort me. I don't cry but, Tom has tears in his eyes.

This moment seems so surreal but it is real. Reality is staring us in our eyes. We have children and we're so young. We don't want to believe the results, but as Dr. Meng assured me, they saw it so it must be true! Right now we both are so numb, not really knowing what needs to be done until the doctors come to explain it to us. We sit and Tom has his arm around me. For once, I'm speechless!

As we wait, out in the hallway I see two male doctors. I just know they are the two who are searching for me, but not because they are wearing white straight jackets or anything of the sort. My humor is still all good, Amen! I know because I happen to see the hospital tags on their jackets stating they are from Neurology. Also I hear my name mentioned by one of them as Sylvia directs them into our room.

They introduce themselves and begin their neurological test. Dr. Jamie Miller begins by telling us Dr. Shapiro will be here in an hour to explain the results of the scan; he is finishing up with a surgery. Dr. Miller then asks a series of questions. He asks, "Kim, do you know why you're here today? Where are we? What day is it? What do you call these?" as he points to his tie and watch. He asks me to apply all my strength against the palm of his hand. He's checking for weakness. He pricks my fingers with a sharp object and asks if I can feel it. He asks me to walk across the room so he can check my balance.

Both doctors ask many other basic questions, all of which I answer correctly. Right after the test Dr. Miller says, "Very good."

The truth remains that in spite of actually passing the test, I still have a brain tumor and I need it to come out. Ouch!

About 30 minutes after the test another physician walks into my room. He introduces himself as Dr. Scott Shapiro. He is the neurosurgeon whom Dr. Meng "just happened" to have contacted to evaluate me. Dr. Meng was surprised that he could even get Dr. Shapiro to see me so quickly, since he is booked up for months. I'm thankful he is able to see me today!

Dr. Shapiro tells Tom and me that he has just finished viewing my scan. He also does more neurological testing and is ready to answer our questions. We ask many questions and then I tell him of the golf ball hit to my head. I even ask if it could be some sort of internal bruising or bleeding from the hit that he sees. He replies, "Kiddo, it's a real tumor and it's quite large. It's not from the golf ball hitting your head." This is our moment of a reality check. He says *it's **real**!*

I ask a few more questions; "Dr. Shapiro, will it definitely need to come out?"

He emphatically replies, "Yes, it will most definitely need to come out."

I ask, "How long will surgery be?

He says, "Five to six hours."

"Is this life threatening?"

He replies, "Anything in your head of that magnitude is a serious situation." I must be in "La La Land" asking him these questions. I suppose it's really a place where people go when they are in disbelief.

41

Now I ask, "How long do you think it's been there?"

He replies, "Probably a year with its size."

This shocks me because just nine months ago I had an emergency surgery because of a gallbladder attack. At that time my physician, Dr. David E. Matthews, told me it was on the verge of gangrene. Wow, now this physician tells me I have a brain tumor! This just blows me away!

Tom asks some questions. "Since you will be using metal plates and screws to hold the skull together, will she go off in the airport scanners?"

I think to myself, "Why in the world is he asking such a question at this time?"

Dr. Shapiro replies with, "I use titanium, and to answer your question, no, it doesn't set off the airport scanners. She can go off only if she'd like to."

Tom asks, "Will the brain compensate for the void after the mass is taken out?"

He then says, "It will fill with cranial pressure. You can literally call her an airhead." We three laugh even though the joke's on me. Dr. Shapiro's and Tom's sense of humor go perfectly with this kind of diagnosis. Laughter is good medicine! I'm a jokester as well and so appreciate the humor at this time.

Tom then asks when Dr. Shapiro thinks the tumor should come out. He replies, "You shouldn't wait!" He then asks if we can have a second opinion. Dr. Shapiro immediately says, "Of course you have that right, *but* don't wait. Get it today or tomorrow at the very latest. This is quite a serious situation!" We thank Dr. Shapiro and head out to deal with the reality and to get a second opinion.

42

I suppose we both are in "La La Land." We just want to wish this all away. Maybe we think by asking one more surgeon it may give us one more chance that it could just go away on its own with no surgery involved?! However, God is in control, not us.

After meeting Dr. Shapiro, I have all the confidence in the world in him. This surgeon exudes a confidence of a sort I've never known before.

CHAPTER | 9

Paths Line Up for Reasons

In all your ways acknowledge Him, and He will direct your paths.

(Proverbs 3:6)

Dr. Meng is a top notch physician who truly cares about the welfare of all his patients, including when one of them has headaches. I am the one who is blessed. I believe God had lined up our paths for reasons unknown to me some 12+ years ago.

As we are getting ready to leave, Sylvia tells us Dr. Meng is on the phone asking to speak with us. He is curious about what Dr. Shapiro's plan of action is. I greet him once again with; "Hi Dr. Meng." I still have a positive attitude because I know that the Lord is in complete control; yet it is a bit scary, I must admit, not knowing what the outcome of all this will be.

I tell Dr. Meng that Dr. Shapiro has confidence in getting this tumor out. But I also tell him about Tom's wanting a second opinion. He says, "I understand."

I have one question in particular and I ask, "Is Dr. Shapiro pretty good?"

Surprised, he asks, "Kim, you and Tom have never heard of him?!"

I reply, "No, but I have heard of Shapiro's Delicatessen."

He says, "No, he's not affiliated with the deli; don't even ask him. Have you heard of Lance Armstrong, the six-time winner of the Tour de France?"

I say, "Yes, of course!"

He then replies, "Dr. Shapiro was Lance's neurosurgeon and successfully removed two tumors from his brain in 1996."

I reply, "He didn't even mention it to us! What a modest man!"

Dr. Meng continues, "Kim, I have no problem with his performing the surgery. I'll go as far as to say he is the *best* in the country!"

I know from Dr. Meng's ultimate confidence in Dr. Shapiro that I will have the best of care. I say, "Nothing but the best for a child of God. Amen!" I could sense Dr. Meng's smile.

CHAPTER | 10

Second Opinion, Please!

After we leave and are in the parking lot, Tom immediately phones our dear friend and surgeon, Dr. Todd Midla, of Atlas Orthopedics and Sports Medicine in Indianapolis and tells him of the news. He is stunned and tells Tom he is sorry. Tom values his opinion and asks if he knows of any more neurosurgeons who are good. When you're dealing with brain tumors, you want the best neurosurgeon possible. Todd tells him of one more and even looks his number up for us.

Since I'm a secretary by occupation, I make the call. He has an opening in his schedule for the next day. What are the chances of that happening?! No coincidence! In the meantime, I have "a lot on my mind," literally. No joke, Ba bomp! And I need to make the necessary calls to my family, not to mention that we will need to tell our children whom I love so dearly! The kids are still young and I don't think they will understand the seriousness of it all so I will have Tom tell them in the most suitable way. He is calm natured and will be able to tell them better than I.

I also think to myself, I have to tell one other person: Matthew, my son who I had prior to meeting Tom. I placed him up for adoption when I gave birth to him 15 years ago. I have to make a necessary call to the adoption agency here in town and ask them to notify his parents. It was an open adoption which means we have the right to keep in touch with him by sending letters through the adoption agency. At this time we have not met but I know his parents' first names; I have to let Bob and Chris know. It is up to them to tell Matthew if they think he should know. I know that God will work it all out.

Side note: Matthew and I will have our grand reunion a year after I recover from this brain surgery. He's met the rest of my side of the family and we all get along great. God lined up all our paths because Matthew's parents were my former youth ministers and I never knew they were the ones God chose. They weren't able to have children the natural way but God chose supernaturally to bless them with a son, one that will carry on their name.

It was the most difficult decision I've ever made in my life! The choice was mine and it was prayerfully made and I continue to trust God in His abundance of grace and faithfulness. I'm just a sinner saved by His amazing grace and forgiveness. God chose to use my older sister, Terri, aka: Teese, to fulfill His blessings for Bob and Chris. Teese chose her dear friends to be his parents. She even took me to the adoption agency for the paperwork. I never knew about the adoptive parents until 16 years later.

What a good secret keeper my sister is! But what she didn't know is it was Chris who introduced Tim and me in the first place. God knew how it would all play out in the journey. It's another "God thing" that continues to happen.

Most recently, Tom, Calvin, Collin, Rachel and Spencer and I made the 8 ½ hour drive to attend Matthew's high school graduation and stayed with Bob and Chris at their invitation for almost a week. God is generous and I'm so grateful!

CHAPTER | 11

Prayer on Bended Knees
Fear Not

As evening arrives, I feel exhausted. I tell Tom I'm going to sleep in Calvin's bed tonight. Not really sure why I chose that room but I think it's because I just wanted to be alone and in peace so I could take it all in with the new issues on my mind.

> *The Lord is my light and my salvation; whom shall I fear?*
>
> (Psalm 27:1)

I attest to this verse once again with first hand knowledge, having walked through the valley many times by now:

> *In all your ways acknowledge Him, and He will make your paths straight.*
>
> (Proverbs 3:6)

I go and do find solace in Calvin's room. I've come here to lie down and I embrace the peacefulness I feel here. I think of many facts about my health and it still seems surreal. I ask myself, "How will this affect my family?" There is a lot of soul-searching going on right now. The fact is that I could die. I mean he did say it was "quite large" and they thought it was cancerous.

Wow, try to count sheep to that!

I need to rest up for my second neurosurgeon's appointment in the morning. I finally fall asleep, praying with "full faith." Now it's morning; at around seven a.m. **something astounding happens!** I awaken to these clearly-heard words in my right ear: "Get on your knees and pray to Me!" I look around and realize no one else is physically in the room and the door is closed. I usually sleep with the door open, but not last night. I knew that voice had to be God's. Later I found this verse in the Bible:

> *And when you pray, do not be like the hypocrites, for they love to pray standing in the synagogues and on the street corners to be seen by men. But when you pray, go into your room, close the door and pray to your Father, who is unseen. Then your Father, who sees what is done in secret, will reward you.*

(Matthew 6:5-8)

For the very first time since the news of my tumor, I break down and really cry. I cry hard! I guess I just find it so difficult to believe it's happening to me. I mean I hear of others having brain tumors, but this time it's my head it's in, not the ones I hear of on the news. I must have just stepped out of that "La La Land and into reality land!"

It is very humbling to know that God wants me just where He has me, on my knees in His very presence. I had not planned on praying in this way on my knees. I was just trying to comprehend that I have the tumor and that it has to come out. But I quickly get to my knees and pray the following:

"Lord I haven't done this since I was a kid, getting on my knees and all."

I hear, "Yes, I know!"

I become a little frightened and say, "Lord, I pray for Your will in my life. I pray for Your complete healing upon my brain."

Right after I send those words up in prayer, my left ear hears, "I want you to touch the area where Dr. Shapiro says your tumor lies."

I do this without any hesitation. I pray that same exact prayer but this time with my right hand upon where the tumor lies. My prayer is with much more conviction this time: "Lord I pray for Your complete healing of my brain!" Heat literally fills the palm of my hand! I'm freaking out! I immediately open my eyes and just look at and feel my palm, trying to figure out how this just happened. I think to myself, "Kim there's no way you could have just caused heat in the palm of your hand on your own. This is all real and this is God, speaking to you!" I continue to lift my left hand in reverence to Him this entire prayer time.

After I wipe my tears, which are running like water in a rapid river, I close my eyes and pray, "Lord, I've never doubted Your existence. I know You are so real. You are the One that got me on my knees before You this morning. Thank You!"

I continue to pray, "Lord, I pray You knock this tumor out of this ballpark!" I open my eyes again for a moment and think these exact words: "Kim, you are praying to the Lord, the Creator. Why are you praying, 'knock this tumor out of the ballpark?' You are crazy!" Later I'll find this in Psalm 139:4: *"Before a word is on my tongue, You know it completely."*

I close my eyes again and pray, "Lord, that's just my zany sense of humor praying that prayer. I have no idea why I just prayed for You to knock this tumor out of the ballpark, but You do. Lord, You

51

knew the words before they even came out of my mouth, so I'll pray it again. 'Lord, I pray You knock this tumor out of this ballpark.'"

This time as I prayed that same prayer, I did it with so much conviction. I motioned with my right thumb, as if I were adamantly telling the tumor to "Get out of here!"

Later on I find that it is written in the Bible exactly as He had put the words into my mouth. I didn't know why in the world I said it, but He does.

I have put My words into your mouth and covered you with the shadow of My hand – I who set the heavens in place, who laid the foundations of the earth, and who says to Zion, 'You are My people.'

(Isaiah 51:16)

With first-hand knowledge and confidence, I say to you, Dear Reader: He does bring peace and comfort to our lowest valleys. We may not think so while it's storming, but after the rain, the sun does shine again.

Next I pray, "Lord, I pray for the best possible neurosurgeon. Lord, I don't know who it will be, but You do. You know exactly who it will be. Lord, I pray that You give me beyond-a-shadow-of-a-doubt wisdom to know whether it will be my second opinion physician today or if it will be Dr. Scott Shapiro to perform my surgery. Please make it known to me in a great and mighty way, so I'll have no doubt."

After that prayer this happens: with my eyes still shut, I literally read this on the front of my forehead: Isaiah 41:10. This totally freaks me out! I run to get my Bible to see what this Scripture is and it says,

So do not fear, for I am with you; do not be dismayed,
for I am your God. I will strengthen you and help you;
I will uphold you with My righteous right hand.

I cried even more after experiencing this! It's something I'll never, ever forget: God's presence!

Talk about something miraculous! Just know that I'm not what one would consider a religious freak. My Bible had recently been collecting dust since I hadn't used it much lately. I don't even know where to find all the books of the Bible. I literally had to go to the front of the Good Book to find out what page Isaiah was on. I know it must mean something because I saw it written with my eyes still closed. This kind of thing hasn't ever happened to me before.

But, something interesting - just a mere five days prior to my diagnosis, I had asked the Lord in prayer to relight the fire that I had had when I was a new Christian. He truly lit me up, bonfire-style with the marshmallows, chocolate bars, and graham crackers to boot! He has my attention now!

I take this as truly an awakening from the Lord to show me how important we are to Him, and that He is listening to us when we pray. I'm learning from this experience that when we place all our faith and trust in His power, we should be ready to expect miraculous things. There is a purpose in this but I don't know what it could be. He knows and I will trust Him!

Side note: When I shared this with my sister Teese, she told me heat signifies healing. I say, **"No way is this all coincidental!"** *This is an experience with God that I can't explain. But it most definitely was undeniably real.*

I'm just an ordinary person who asked Jesus into my life and asked for His forgiveness of my sins and I try to live a decent life. I'm His daughter. Nahum 1:7b says, "He cares for those who trust in Him."

What is impossible with men is possible with God.
(Luke 18:27)

I literally sum this up as a "God thing" for sure!

CHAPTER | 12

Second Opinion Physician Visit

JUNE 28, 2003

It's now 1:00 p.m. and Tom is driving me to my appointment with the other highly recommended neurosurgeon. My appointment is for 1:30 p.m. so we are making great time. The kids are staying with Tom's sister. What a blessing she is in our time of need!

We arrive and I sign in at the front desk. We find a place to sit and begin to read magazines.

While sitting, I begin with praying in my mind that God would show me beyond a shadow of a doubt whether it will be this doctor or if it will be Dr. Shapiro. Neurologists and neurosurgeons are most definitely gifted with bright brains in their line of work. It's a God-given talent which each is blessed to have. Speaking for all of us patients diagnosed with brain tumors, I'm thankful for all these surgeons who have been there and done that. I feel there's hope after all!

There are different kinds of gifts, but the same Spirit.
There are different kinds of service, but the same Lord.

There are different kinds of workings, but the same God works all of them in all men.

(1 Corinthians 12:4-6)

The nurse calls my name. We are escorted to a room and meet with the neurosurgeon. We greet each other and he begins the process of interpreting the scan. Having my inquisitive mind, I start asking questions as I did with Dr. Shapiro. I ask, "What type of tumor is it, and does it have a scientific name? How do you think I got it in the first place?"- things of that nature. I tell him I like to know these kinds of facts.

He says, "Kim, you'll just confuse yourself, so just leave the scientific names to us."

He then asks me to walk across the room so he can check my balance. Still having my zany sense of humor, I boldly say, "So, you want me to do a cat walk like models?"

He looks stoically at me and says, "Kim, just walk across the room for me."

I think, "Hmm, this isn't going as well as it did with Dr. Shapiro." As I mentally keep track between Dr. Shapiro and this neurosurgeon, I think to myself: *"At least Dr. Shapiro has a great sense of humor. I mean, really, I'm the one with the tumor and the humor!"*

At least I get some of the questions answered. But when I ask how long my surgery will be, he replies, "two or three hours." When I ask how he thinks it got there in the first place. He says, "By chance."

I'm sorry, but, "By chance!" I don't buy that answer. I need another vowel. Please! My "red flags" were rising the more he and I spoke to each other. Big difference in the surgery duration, and also his bedside manner!

56

The more he and I talk the more I feel uneasy with this surgeon. He leaves the room to get some literature for us to take home. While he is out of the room for the moment, I motion off to the side with my right hand to Tom by shaking my fingertips in a "most definite no" gesture. I really feel each time I have a question I can't ask it because the doctor cuts me off by dodging each question.

He returns to the room with the *American Brain Tumor Association Primer of Brain Tumors - A Patient's Reference Manual*. In the most respectful and polite way I say to him, "I guess I'll just zip it up and not ask any more questions!"

He replies, "You don't have to 'zip it up,' just leave the technical stuff to us."

My attitude is: "Hey, it's my brain, my tumor and my mind requesting answers. They deal with tumors day in and day out, but this is my tumor. Of course, I'm curious! I have a gut feeling that he isn't going to be the one the Lord has planned for my surgery."

I now ask him when he thinks my surgery will need to take place. His reply surprises me. He says, "You might want to wait until after the July 4th holiday weekend. Many people have annual plans then."

I reply, "I have no plans, but I do want to have the surgery!" I take his comment to mean that he is the one with the annual plans.

My mind is thinking of what Dr. Shapiro had said the day before about how he doesn't want to wait to perform the surgery. But this surgeon's first available appointment is after the "holiday weekend" and will be July 8th. I will be a *mere* "work in" on the second surgeon's appointment list.

Yes, God has plans for me to be a "work-in progress." This is true!

57

After the appointment, we head back home. As we pull into the garage and I open the door to the kitchen the phone rings as if it knows we just walked in. I answer it on the second ring and it is Pam from Dr. Shapiro's office. She says, "Dr. Shapiro has called the office twice to inquire how your second opinion went."

I tell her, "Pam, Tom and I just walked in the door from that appointment." As God is our witness, and He most certainly is, Pam tells me about a cancellation in Dr. Shapiro's booked-up schedule for July 3, 2003, the holiday weekend. God is working overtime miracles. Just maybe that other person scheduled for the surgery time was an angel holding a place for me. The Lord never ceases to amaze us!

She continued, "If you choose him, he wants to meet with you this Wednesday to go over any and all questions you may have before surgery. And, he wants to perform surgery on Thursday, the next day. He doesn't want to wait!" I know with great certainty that with this call from Pam, God has shown me beyond a shadow of a doubt that Dr. Shapiro will be my neurosurgeon.

I say, "Pam, sign me up!" You see, she has no idea about my prayer, but I have my answer now. God knows how important it is for me to have this information. It will most certainly be Dr. Scott Shapiro who will be the one to perform the miracle that the Lord is sending.

CHAPTER | 13

Wednesday's Appointment with Dr. Shapiro

MORNING OF JULY 2, 2003

The time is here and we are at the appointment with Dr. Shapiro. He is ready to answer our questions; I am better able to ask my questions. I begin with a bold statement to him: "Dr. Shapiro, I'm looking forward to my surgery in the morning. Has anyone ever said that to you before her or his surgery?"

He looks at me with a big smile and says, "Kiddo, not in those exact words." We ask other questions. Tom and I know positively that the Lord is in complete control of this surgery and the rest of my life. We know that with this neurosurgeon, we're in the best of hands. No worries! He tells us before we leave, "Get some good rest tonight because you are going to need it for your big day tomorrow!"

I make a comment to the effect of: "don't work too late tonight. We will definitely see you in the morning." We all smile.

Tom and I feel at peace despite the surgery in less than 24 hours. God lined up the paths of these doctors and I most certainly feel Dr. Shapiro was hand-chosen by God! Dr. Shapiro's God-given talents have helped so many who were in this same situation. Lance Armstrong, whose two tumors Dr. Shapiro successfully removed, has now gone where no man has been before with the Tour de France. Lance did, and I'm about to get the best neurosurgeon for our brains, as did the countless others whose surgeries have been performed by him. I speak on behalf of all his former patients, "We are thankful and extremely grateful for the expertise and talent that make him the superb neurosurgeon he is!"

CHAPTER | 14

Preparing for Praise!

AFTERNOON OF JULY 2, 2003

Here are a couple of interesting things that are happening: my sister Amy and I are picking our sister Teese up at the Indianapolis Airport. She wants to be with us during the surgery. Her husband Mark, our niece Anne and nephew Mark will be here in a couple of days. As we are awaiting Teese's arrival, Amy and I take a short stroll in some of the airport shops. We walk past a sunglasses shop and I am stunned to see to our right, a poster displayed in a metal freestanding frame at the entrance. This poster almost seems to be trying to get my attention. But Amy walks past it, not even noticing it.

When I spot it, I see it is a cyclist wearing a helmet and sporting some cool-looking sunglasses which this store sells. As I look in the store more intensely I notice there are six more posters hanging on their walls. I turn to Amy and say, "Look, it's Lance Armstrong. He's on all the posters."

Amy says, "Ok, so he is." To her it wasn't a big deal, but to me it was. I've been having many "coincidental" things happening and here is the most successful Tour de France winner. I view it as a big puzzle and I've just found one more piece of it. I'm thinking: "all right, no way!" I see it literally *as a sign* **from God** *in more ways*

than one that everything is going to be just fine. I mean look at how Lance has overcome his battle with cancer and it was right here at the Indiana Cancer Center at Indiana Medical Center. Dr. Shapiro was his neurosurgeon seven years ago!

I tell Amy that seven years ago he had the same neurosurgeon that will operate on me tomorrow. She says, "That's good!" I explain to her that these posters give me a better sense of hope. And it also reassures me that brain tumors aren't always **death** sentences. Amy says, "All right, but please don't use that ***death*** word again."

I think Amy and the rest of my family are scared because it is brain surgery! She may think I'm on some sort of drug to keep my nerves calm, but I'm not. I tell her, "I know I'm in the best of care with my neurosurgeon! I feel confident that I will be the next miracle. Now Sis, it's quite doubtful that I will ever win a Tour de France, but I will be a winner in other ways in this journey we call, 'life!'"

She says, "That's right! Keep your great attitude!" Soon, I too will be celebrating a most successful ride in my journey. She and I hug and it is now time for Teese's plane to be here.

She arrives and we all hug; it's like a family reunion. She and her husband Mark lived in the town of Cicero, Indiana until Mark had a job transfer to West Palm Beach, Florida. Teese says, "You don't have to have such a serious operation for me to fly to visit you."

I say, "I know you'd come any time and visit. Thank you for coming back so soon." She was just here visiting over Spring Break a couple months ago. I also tell her I've already notified the agency so they can call Matt's parents and tell them of the news. She says that was a good idea. She also mentions that she doesn't think Matt should meet me under this circumstance. She feels assured that surgery will be successful and that God will allow us to have our grand reunion. I tell her I agree and I'm hopeful we will all get to meet Matt.

CHAPTER | 15

Karaoke Night Before Surgery

JULY 2, 2003 LATE AFTERNOON
AND INTO EVENING

After we pack Teese's bags in the back of the car we head to my home so she can get unpacked and settle into "her new home" with us. I had received a message from the adoption agency while we were at the airport; I had left my cell phone in the car. So I phone them and I am told they had received an overnight letter for me. I suggest to Amy, "Let's go and get it," and ask "will you drive?" We three drive there in anticipation of what the letter will say.

The letter and pictures I had received are the most precious thing. All three of us cry tears of joy as we look at Matt's wonderful pictures. I have a peace knowing they, too, are praying for me during my journey through this valley. I know for sure that we will meet one day and it won't be during my time in the valley, but when I'm well again.

In the letter they write to tell me that Matthew is a Christian and is strong in his faith for a youth of his age, knowing this would bring much-needed comfort at this time for me. I'm blessed beyond measure.

63

EVENING BEFORE SURGERY

I'm thinking about trying out the new karaoke machine Tom just bought. Amy and Teese have beautiful voices and I think it will be a lot of fun. I wonder if they might be up to singing?! I am and I know Tom probably will be, too. I mean, tomorrow will be a big day but why not sing and celebrate tonight?! I'm up for it. It's just brain surgery. Oh yeah, *just* brain surgery.

It's just the four of us here tonight since the kids are staying with our family until after I get home from surgery. We gather in our living room around the TV and the karaoke machine. We begin praying over my surgery which will take place in less than 24 hours. We pray for God to guide Dr. Shapiro's hands accurately according to His will.

After we pray a while we begin to sing without music or the karaoke machine. We are winging it a cappella. We sing praise and worship songs. We start out by singing "Amazing Love, Amazing Grace," and then Teese turns to Amy and says, "Amy, I think you have a song in you."

Side note here: Amy and Teese both are gifted singers.

Amy then turns to Teese with a question in her tone of voice and says, "I do? What might that be?"

Teese says, "His eye is on the Sparrow."

Amy says, "I don't know all the verses."

Teese says, "That's all right. We'll look it up on the computer." And they do, and print the words; she sings them most beautifully. As I just mentioned, Amy and Teese are both gifted with their voices. Their voices are like angels singing in my ears.

64

God gives all of us gifts and talents and their voices are among the many gifts Amy and Teese have. "This is the Lords' Day"; I shall rejoice and be glad that it happens to have been the next song on our minds. I will sing it on my own, come tomorrow morning!

We all agree it's getting late and we need sleep so we can be well rested come morning. My sisters sleep at our home and the kids are already at their cousins'. What a day tomorrow will be! I'm ready for it! Good Night. It's now approximately 11:00 p.m. and you know where I am.

Despite the surgical circumstance which awaits me in the morning, I actually sleep well. I have no doubt I will be well taken care of!

"Are not two sparrows sold for a penny? Yet not one of them will fall to the ground apart from the will of your Father. And even the very hairs of your head are all numbered. So don't be afraid; you are worth more than many sparrows" (Matthew 10:29-31).

"When troubles and sickness come our way, we usually turn to worry and fretting about our situation." Civilla Martin (1869-1948), the author of today's hymn had a friend who had learned to rely on this verse when, in 1904, sickness made her bedridden and she continued to trust in God. Seeing the testimony of her friend caused Civilla Martin to pen the words to our hymn,

HIS EYE IS ON THE SPARROW

Why should I feel discouraged,
Why should the shadows come...
When Jesus is my portion?
My constant Friend is He;

His eye is on the sparrow,
and I know He watches me...
Source: http://schaefer-family.com/hymns/sparrow.htm

CHAPTER | 16

Surgery Morning

JULY 3, 2003

I get up, shower and shave my legs. I even put blush and eye make up on in preparation for the hospital visit. I was instructed not to eat anything after midnight last night and I didn't. I guess they don't want me getting sick during the surgery. I wear my favorite black and pink shirt with black pants. It's now time to leave and head for I U Medical. Tom drives and we talk some more. I just feel really at peace this morning. Can't really explain it any other way but to say it's a "God thing." Tom agrees.

We arrive promptly at 9 a.m. and register at the front desk. This will be a memorable day in our lives. I look around and see many family members here as well as more than two dozen folks from our church. They make me know I'm loved. We hug and thank them all for being here for our event of a lifetime. They are a family that we have grown to love and appreciate since we joined our church many years ago. Our minister, Jim Burks, his wife Laura, daughter Deanna, and son David are a true Godsend. We see God working in great and mighty ways in the church.

I have many stops to make before the surgery. We sit and pray and all hold hands. It is a testimony in itself for a church to bond together as we do. Many plan to stay for the duration of the projected five-to-six hour surgery. Tom's sister says she is planning to get egg rolls and other Vietnamese finger foods for all who are waiting. We are so blessed with a big loving family!

After we pray, the nurses from the operating room come to prepare me for the next leg of this journey. They say, "Kim, there are a lot of people out there who love you."

I reply, "Yes, it's our family and our church family as well."

One nurse comments, "Many people come in here with no one but themselves. You have many folks here who love you and it shows." She is right! I am loved and it feels great!

They send me to be prepped for the brain mapping. This involves little round disks called fiducials. They are placed on different points of my head so they can strategically guide this three-dimensional stealth technology. Its purpose is to map exactly where the tumor lies so that they can get the entire tumor plus any "hidden" cells. It also entails Cheryl's using the razor for the first time to shave off clumps of my hair. I'm so thankful for all this technology!

CHAPTER | 17

Waiting Room Before Surgery

After Cheryl glued the fiducials to my skin and scalp, Tom, my sister-in-law, Kim Nguyen (yes there are two of us) and I go to a pre-surgery waiting area. As we are sitting there, I ask Tom, "Hon, could you please get me my bag? I want to put on the lotion that Butch and Anne gave me yesterday."

After I put it on, my new attending nurse, Linda, comes into the waiting area. She makes a comment about how wonderful the lotion smells. I tell her it is from our neighbors, and it is Cotton Blossom by Bath and Body Works. She says, "It has such a fresh clean smell to it."

I say, "Well, Linda, I am getting ready for brain surgery. I want to smell good going in." *I add*, "Feel free to put some on if you like." She thanks me and begins to squeeze some sparingly out into her hands. I look at her and say, "Nurse Linda, use it as if it were on your dresser at home." She smiles and tells me that "every time" she smells this scent she will think of me. She has such a wonderful presence. Her smile is truly amazing. It's genuine and brings much comfort to my situation.

Just now I realize my monthly cycle has started. Oh, no! Maybe my body is just on overload. I turned and ask Linda if the hospital would happen to have some pads. I add, "What a day, brain surgery and my period all at the same time. What more could a woman want?!" She smiles and goes to get what I need.

Now Nurse Roxanne arrives and says, "It sure smells good in here!"

I reply, "Thank you." I tell her it's Cotton Blossom. "Would you like to put some on, too? Help yourself." She does. I say to her as I have said to Nurse Linda: "I'm getting ready to go into my brain surgery and I want to smell good."

She replies, "You do!"

CHAPTER | 18

Boldness Before Brain Surgery

Not too long after that, Dr. Jamie Miller, the same intern whom I met in Dr. Meng's office less than a week ago, walks into the now-scented room. He is here to repeat a neurological exam just prior to the surgery. He begins by asking the questions he asked before. "Can you count backwards from 20 for me? Do you know where you are today and why you are here? What is today's date?" He asks many other questions, and once again, I pass with flying colors. Guess I'm still a good candidate for surgery.

Side note: After surgery I shall ask Dr. Shapiro who cut my hair. He will tell me it was Dr. Miller. I was just curious who has to do that part of the surgery. It's my curious mind!

After the neurological exam, I boldly say, "Dr. Miller, you're so kind and compassionate, I bet you're married!"

He quickly replies, "Yes, very!"

I tell him, "I'm always looking out for my single younger sister, Amy. She works with a wonderful bunch of ladies at Met Life. I hope you don't think my question was crazy!"

His reply: "No, I find it quite flattering." After the exam, he leaves my room and takes his notes so he can prepare for the beginning of my surgery. Hope he didn't include the marriage part in his notes. I bet he didn't for sure.

Side note: I'll run into him later while waiting at the elevator for one of my regular MRI scans. He thinks I am doing great and will say the incision is healing just as it should. I'll tell him about my writing of this book and I'll ask if I may include the marital question I asked him just prior to my going into surgery. He will say, "Of course you may. I give my permission."

CHAPTER | 19

My Defining Moment

For where two or three come together in My name, there am I with them.

(Matthew 18:20)

Next, just prior to my going into the actual operating room, a man walks into my room. He says, "Are you Kim Nguyen?"

I say, "Why, yes, I am." He introduces himself as Michael Beaumont, the worship pastor of Kingsway Christian Church.

"You are on the prayer list and I want to pray with you. I've had such a hard time locating you but they finally directed me to the right place!" *I am on their list because Calvin, Collin and Rachel go to their God-talented school.*

I tell him, "Michael, it is God's perfect timing because in just a little while I'm going in for surgery. The Lord will perform a miracle. I just know He will!" He talks a little with Tom, Kim and me. We all hold hands and he leads us into a prayer, then we all say a prayer and I close it. I thank the Lord for being such an awesome God and for His timing which allowed Michael to find me. God is awesome and His timing is always perfect.

I will be glad and rejoice in Your love, for You saw my affliction and knew the anguish of my soul. You have not

*handed me over to the enemy but have set my feet in a
spacious place.*

(Psalm 31:7-8)

*Side note: After I have surgery and am back home I shall call
Michael and ask him to write his thoughts about what he remembers
from our time together just moments before the surgery. I'll tell him
of my desire to write a book of my experience because it's all about
the ultimate Him, not Kim. He will write the thoughts that impacted
him that day that I will share with you now:*

"I was impressed by the strength of Kim's faith. Many times
making hospital calls, you walk into rooms where the levity of the
situation is palpable. Most of those instances suck the faith out of
people. If they express their hope and faith, it is usually spoken with
fear or desperation.

"But when I walked into your room, your faith was not spoken
as a last hope, but as a first line of defense and support. Initially I
thought, 'This poor woman doesn't realize how serious this situation
is!' But my mind and heart were quickly changed at the realization
that I didn't realize how serious God's promises and faithfulness are.

"Kim's faith overwhelmed me as we prayed together. It was as
if there was no doubt in her mind (and I believe that there was no
doubt) that she was going to be healed. During our prayer, it was
obvious that God was present because He is faithful to those who are
faithful to Him. I remember that she was thrilled to have the same
surgeon working with her who had worked with world champion
cyclist Lance Armstrong. Truth be told, while I am sure he is an
incredible physician, Kim was worked on by the Great Physician,
and so was I."

CHAPTER | 20

The Time Arrives

It is now time to get ready, set and go! I am now heading into the operating room; Nurse Roxanne checks my blood pressure as the normal protocol goes. It is 104/60 with 100% oxygen level. She finds it hard to believe, so she re-checks the readings and makes sure they are correct. It still registers 104/60 with 100% oxygen level. She says, "Wow, Kim you are calm!"

I reply, "I have the peace of God that passes all understanding and He's present with us now."

"Now, where in the world did that come from?" I'm thinking. I can say I feel His presence and know His peace. He's real and I say this confidently with first-hand knowledge!

Because of the positive attitude I have going into the six-hour brain surgery, Linda says, "Kim you are so awesome."

Quickly I reply, "Nurse Linda, the Lord is the awesome one, I'm just His daughter. I guess since He is the King, I'm a princess." She also asks me what is in the middle of the cross necklace I am wearing.

I tell her, "It's a mustard seed. The Bible tells us if we have faith as small as this mustard seed that we can move mountains. Don't you know I have that much faith and so much more? He has it all under control. You just wait and see. He's getting ready to move this mountain right out of my noggin."

She says, "We've never had anyone in the OR with an attitude as positive as yours, especially going into brain surgery! It will only help with your recovery after surgery."

I tell her and Roxanne, "I like to bake and I will make you guys some cookies when I get home."

They say, "Kim, we just want you to get better so don't even worry about the cookies; we do appreciate the thought though."

Side note here: I shall surprise the operation room nurses with a variety of 12 dozen cookies about a month after my surgery, along with an inspirational card which they will hang up in the break room for all to read. I made the offer and kept my promise. She and Roxanne will be amazed that I would do such a thing.

Another side note: It is John Ryder, our Sunday school leader who taught us a lesson on the mustard seed parable while at Clermont Christian Church. He told us, "It's very interesting because the mustard seed is the smallest seed that produces the largest tree." I've always been fascinated by this story during youth group discussions since I was a youngster growing up in the church.

Linda says, "Kim, it's time for your surgery so I'll talk to you later. You've been a joy and a breath of fresh air around here." The last thing I recall is her smiling at me and the comfort I have walking into surgery.

I tell her and Roxanne, "Remember, God is the awesome one not I!"

Mustard seed parable:

I tell you the truth, if you have faith as small as a mustard seed, you can say to his mountain, 'Move from here to there' and it will move. Nothing will be impossible for you.

(Matthew 17:20)

CHAPTER | 21

Operating Room Miraculous Experience

Miracle: 1: an extraordinary event manifesting divine intervention in human affairs, source *Merriam Webster Dictionary*

"You are about to witness a miracle" is what I boldly proclaim to our dear church friend Brenda Popp just as I go into surgery. She is blessed with the gift of giving comfort in difficult times, not to mention that God has blessed her with her career and expertise in electro-neuro diagnostics.

While I am lying on the operating table, something unfathomable occurs. I literally am brain storming and thinking, "Kim, the surgery is just about to happen!" I am excited and very observant of my surroundings.

I even hear two nurses talking about me, "Does she know what she's in here for?"

The other nurse covers her mouth and says, "Yes, she does!"

The first nurse says, "Wow!" Well, I guess they don't think I am paying attention to them. But, oh, I am. They just don't know how observant I am, brain tumor or not! I am thankful that I was able to witness that exchange.

I am amazed at how clean and brightly lit this huge room is. There are so many people present to assist with the surgery, each of them having a role and playing a part in this miracle that is about to take place because of the Lord's ultimate blueprint for this procedure. As for the two nurses, they may have just witnessed the faith and trust I have in the middle of my storm. I hope I was the Lord's witness.

Although I'm in the middle of a storm and it's lightning while I struggle in the shadow of this deadly valley, I know the sun will shine again. The rainbow is always beautiful after the storm and I continue to trust Him!

To my left, I see and hear a nurse moving sterile metal instruments around in a huge steel basin. The clinking noises are fearsome to me. It somewhat resembles the fear one has while on a roller-coaster ride. At the top of the highest point, before the drop, a heart just sinks. Well, that's kind of how I'm feeling at this time.

Frightening reality in the making, but it will be alright because of God's miracle. I feel the need to turn my head away from all that noise. Remember, my mind is usually inquisitive, but **definitely** not this time.

I need to close my eyes to gather a calm during this storm. I lay my head to my right and once again, I pray. This time I pray, "Lord, fill me with Your peace. The same peace You've filled me with up until now."

Now something else remarkable happens. I hear audibly the following through my right ear: "I want you to touch Dr. Shapiro's hands before surgery and tell him I will be using his hands and his eyes as My instruments to get every 'minute' piece of tumor from your brain, *but* I'm the One performing the operation."

"Minute" isn't even in my vocabulary. The Bible tells us that He knows His children by name and He knows what we will say even before we say it. I know that's true. I am ever so thankful for my Supreme Neurosurgeon and His blessed work through Dr. Scott Shapiro and Dr. Jamie Miller!

Know that the Lord is God. It is He who made us, and we are His; we are His people, the sheep of His pasture.
(Psalm 100:3)

...He calls His own sheep by name and leads them out.
(John 10:3)

I look up to the ceiling and say out loud, "Wow, Lord, that's heavy." Probably no one else in the OR is listening to my comment, but I know the Lord is. If anyone else is listening, he or she must think I've lost my mind. I anticipate and watch for my neurosurgeon to come into the OR so I can tell him the awesome news.

Side note here: I find that the protocol of surgery is that the surgeon comes in after the patient has been prepped for surgery and thus already knocked out by the medication.

As I lie and wait to share this news I hear the door opening and footsteps coming toward me. Then I hear, "Hello, I'm Dr. Keever, I will be your anesthesiologist today."

I look up and say, "Dr. Keever, you were my anesthesiologist nine months and one day ago when my gallbladder was removed by Dr. David E. Matthews."

Looking stunned, he replies, "My, you remember me?"

I say, "Yes, I remember you."

He replies, "Was I any good?"

I reply, "Yes, you did a great job, I don't remember anything else, but I remember you."

The nurse says, "Kim that's amazing because no one remembers those guys. They are the ones who knock you out." It is pretty wild that I get him again and I'm quite thankful.

Once again I step out of my comfort zone and say, "Dr. Keever, I've been a Christian since I was eight years old. And I've been talking to Him and He's not calling me home yet. I just thought I'd let you know." Keep in mind, I've had no drugs yet.

His eyes meet mine as he replies, "Kim that's good to know! He smiles and I smile back. I then tell him of my blood pressure and oxygen level. He says, "My Kim, you are awfully calm."

I reply, "Yes, I'm cool as a cucumber."

He says, "Yes, you are a cucumber."

After that I say, "Dr. Keever, I have the peace of God" and Dr. Keever finishes my sentence: "that passes all understanding."

Surprised, I look up and say, "Dr. Keever, have I said it that much?"

He has a huge smile and says, "Just a few times now, Kim."

I then say to Dr. Keever and the other physicians' and nurses, "This is not Kim Nguyen lying here, going into a six-hour brain surgery. I have God's peace that passes all understanding. You don't know why my blood pressure is 104/60 and my oxygen level is at 100%! I do, and I know the Lord is here with us in this very room." I then say, "Dr. Keever, I bet you might be thinking 'knock her out' and get this tumor out of her brain and into its tomb. She's crazy."

We all smile and they proceed with the prepping before Dr. Shapiro and Dr. Miller come in.

A little time goes by and Dr. Keever adjusts my lines to get ready to stick my veins with the knockout meds. But he looks puzzled. I ask, "What's wrong?"

He says, "Your veins are slippery."

I say, "What can I do to help?"

He replies, "Just relax."

I take a deep breath and exhale and say, "How's that now?"

He says, "Actually, good!" I ask how long I'll be "out," and he replies, "As long as it takes." That is the very last thing I shall remember asking him, as I count out loud "one, two…" and in no time flat, I am out. I bet Dr. Keever is pleased with my silence for the moment, for a lot of moments.

Next is the six-hour surgery for which he has prepped me. The worry part is gone. Present with us in the operating room is the Lord God Almighty, exuding His undeniable peace. I wish I could hear what everyone is saying now.

> *…Therefore I tell you, do not worry about your life…Who of you by worrying can add a single hour to his life?*
>
> (Matthew 6:25-27)

> *For it will not be you speaking, but the Spirit of your Father speaking through you.*
>
> (Matthew 10:20)

> *Now may the Lord of peace Himself give you peace at all times and in every way. The Lord be with all of you.*
>
> (2 Thessalonians 3:16)

83

And the peace of God, which transcends all understanding, will guard your hearts and your minds in Christ Jesus.

(Philippians 4:7)

"Peace" is a state of being quiet according to *Webster's Dictionary.*

Be still, and know I am God...

(Psalm 46:10)

CHAPTER 22

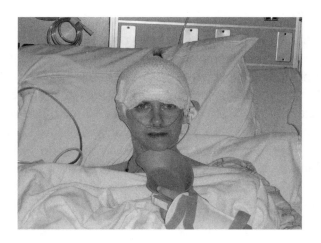

A Jewish Paradox (Pair of Docs)

Six hours later surgery is a success! After I regain consciousness, Dr. Shapiro appears at my bedside. His words come into focus: "Kiddo, surgery went smooth as silk."

Looking up at him, I smile! Still, I don't know how I look or how my head is bandaged and I say, "Dr. Shapiro, silk is pretty smooth!"

We both laugh and he says, "Yes, Kiddo, it went that smoothly." Keep in mind; he doesn't yet know about what the Lord revealed to me while I was on the operating room table.

Side note here: I don't tell him today for some reason but I do tell him on October 16, 2003 when I see him at the Tour of Hope. God's timing is always perfect and that's why I shall tell him during this event when it comes to Indianapolis approximately three months after my surgery. More about that later.

Dr. Shapiro then says, "I've got you three pretty blue bonnets compliments of the hospital and I have one on your head now." First of all, being an observant patient, I thought, "Nothing is complimentary. I'll be billed for it later. See I still have my zany sense of humor minus the tumor now!" He then cuts off the white turban-styled head bandage and throws it into a receptacle, saying, "I think you need to sport your new hairdo. You ladies nowadays can do wonders with hair. I think it will be very healthful for you to look in the mirror at yourself. We had to cut off a little more hair than you and I had anticipated while in my office yesterday."

I reply, "What do you mean; you had to cut off more hair?" At this point, I am thinking, "Ok, how bad could I look?"

He says, "Kiddo, we had to cut more hair because of the size of the tumor."

"How big was it?" I quickly ask.

He says, "It was quite large. He taps my right forearm three times with his right hand and says, "It was literally the size of a baseball. You had fluid on the brain because of the tremendous amount of pressure the tumor placed upon your brain. You brain was literally shifted bilaterally as well."

Side note here: I share the prayer, that I prayed in Calvin's room when I had asked God to, "knock this tumor out of the ballpark," with our friend Jon Hendren. Jon says: "Hey, Kim isn't it three strikes and you're out?" Jon is the owner of the deli which I will just happen to meet my second neurosurgeon's assistant, Dr. Robert Sloan as well as his mom. You will read of this later. Talk about coincidences, no way!

After Dr. Shapiro tells me its size, my first thought is, "Lord, **THAT'S** what You meant when I prayed that prayer in Calvin's room when You got me to my knees. You knew exactly the words before they came out of my mouth as well as Dr. Shapiro's words to me just now." As you may recall I prayed this: "Lord, I pray You knock this tumor out of the ballpark." This is my revelation: my tumor was the baseball and the ballpark is my brain! This is when I decide I need to write a book about my experience of this stormy journey in my life. The baseball size is far too coincidental to be mere coincidence.

Now I'm thinking, "This has to be a book so others can see that ordinary people can be used by God who is extraordinary, and that for sure He is real!" This is ironic because I'm not even a book reader let alone a writer. I'm thinking maybe God meant for this story to be a home run for Him. And to give evidence that each of us has a destiny and a purpose on this earth! It is said that coincidences are God's way of remaining anonymous.

Lying in my bed I say to Dr. Shapiro, "Wow, how could I have not known all that was happening up there?"

He says, "You must have a high pain tolerance."

I say, "Yes, I suppose I do because I've given birth to four of the five of my children without epidurals."

He replies, "Kiddo, the headache you had that woke you up after the golf ball hit was literally your 'wake up' call. Your cranial pressure had reached its peak and that's what you were experiencing with the headache. I'm glad you woke up!"

I reply, "You and me both."

Being quite a jokester, Dr. Shapiro says, "Your husband can literally now call you an 'air head' since your brain will be filling back up with cranial pressure." Tom smiled! Oh, how blessed we are to have been on the same path with this wonderful surgeon in my life's journey.

We laugh and I hug and thank him for all he's done for us. His humor is helping with the reality of having just had my head opened up. He says, "Today is Thursday. I'm going to have you out of here on Sunday."

I say, "But, Dr. Shapiro, that's only four days. We have four wonderful children waiting at home for me. I love them dearly, but I don't want to go home, yet! Are you sure I'll be fine?"

He replies, "You're doing fantastic for someone who's just had brain surgery."

I reply, "Really?"

He emphatically answers, "Yes, just the fact that you're up walking on your own and the fact you are talking is tremendous."

As if I had another reply to get him to keep me longer here in the hospital! I say, "Okay, if you say so!" I must admit, it is nice to be waited on hand and foot.

"I have no doubt you'll do just fine at home!"

Dr. Shapiro points to Tom and says, "Say, I hear this young man is taking you to Hawaii."

I reply, "Oh, I told Tom years ago that I'll see it when we're in Heaven."

He looks at Tom and says, "Was it supposed to be a surprise?" Tom just smiles at him. I brush it off as Dr. Shapiro's humorous side. It is a nice thought though: Hawaii. Of course, there will be more on that subject later.

I do go and look at my "new do" in the bathroom mirror as he suggests. First I see my head is half shaved and I have what looks like a backwards question mark on my noggin. There's a hole in my head, from the drainage tube I'm told. I can feel it but I don't really see it because it's on the back of my head. I'm in awe over all the staples that are holding me together.

Side note: Our surgeon friend Todd Midla visits after I'm allowed visitors and he counts the staples and says, "Kimmie you have 39."

The staples remind me of a baseball with its stitching. I could be a body double for Demi Moore if they ever make another G.I. Jane movie.   But that's after they staple up my stomach, too.   It has stretched because of all the babies I've birthed. Maybe just the head shot could be used for Demi's double.

Wow, it is truly amazing that the tumor is literally out of the ball-park now. Dr. Shapiro says, "You'll always have a question on your mind." He was right and it is healthful for me to see the results of the surgery. Not only will I have a question mark scar on my skull, but I will be able to use it as a means of sharing with others what God has done for me with His mercy and grace.

Dr. Shapiro says the pathologist report shows that my right temporal lobe tumor is a low grade, benign Oligodendroglioma Astrocytoma. I ask him, "In laymen terms, what does that mean?"

He replies, "It means your tumor was classified as being non-cancerous because of the low grade. And you will not need to have chemo or radiation treatments. You will be monitored with an MRI every three months for up to two years." Of course, Tom and I are thrilled that it isn't cancer! I hug Dr. Shapiro one last time and Tom shakes his hand again and we thank him for all he has done. What a decent and humble man!

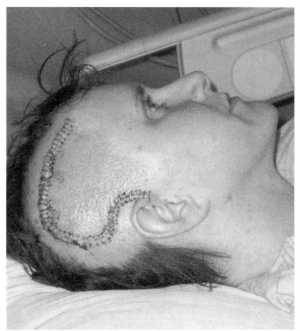

Dr. Shapiro tells me he thinks I need to sport my new hair do.

CHAPTER 23

Comedy Within a Craniotomy

WHAT IS A CRANIOTOMY?

A craniotomy is an operation, or surgery, on the brain. The surgeon makes an opening in the skull so that an operation on the brain can be performed. A craniotomy may be done in any area of the skull, and may be almost any size. When the surgeon is finished operating on the brain, the piece of bone initially removed is usually replaced, so no soft spot is left. (American Brain Tumor Associations website: www.abta.org)

Just after surgery, it is my nurse Mark who takes care of me. Not only do I appreciate his kindness and compassion, but I note that he is the one who removes the drainage tube from my skull. He does it so skillfully that I don't even know he is up to anything. Much like when, as children, our parents pull our loose baby teeth. He distracts me so I'll focus elsewhere and, viola, the tube is out. I say, "Mark, why did you have to do it that way? That hurt!"

He replies, "Kim, believe me, it is best to do it that quickly. It's similar to when you remove a band-aid; you do it quickly rather than feel the pain slowly."

I reply, "Thank you Mark! I understand."

The drainage tube is now out of my skull and I am taken to my recovery room. My brother-in-law, Tim, comes in and says, "Kim, do you remember anything from surgery?"

I reply in a French accent and phrase, "Je ne sais pas."

He is taken aback and says, "Did you take French in high school?"

I answer, "No. I don't know where that came from." I must say this is amazing! I suppose I just picked up that phrase somewhere.

Next, our dear friends Dave and Debbie come to visit. Being a genial by nature, in his deep, natural voice, much like a radio announcer's, Dave asks, "So, Kim, how ya feeling?"

I break out and start to sing the infamous James Brown classic, "I feel good, na, na, na, na, na, na. The way that I should now, Baby. I feel good, so good...."

He immediately says, "Kim we'll have to have a karaoke night at church sometime and I'll sign you up as a participant!"

I know my singing right after surgery must have caught him and Debbie off guard. I know Tom is looking at me in bewilderment. I tell Tom, "Hon, I'm just being funny. Don't worry!" I call this chapter "Comedy within a Craniotomy" because I truly believe laughter is the best medicine.

Side note: *After the surgery and the resting I was moved to my recovery room. I was quick to notice I had one with a great outside view. I thought to myself, "Good, a room with a view." I was able to view the Indianapolis fireworks on July 4th and celebrate with the rest of Indiana my successful surgery the day before.*

Our family and more friends visit with me during the next three days. On the fourth day we leave just as Dr. Shapiro has planned. We are instructed that I will be monitored every three months with an MRI scan. I will also be placed on an anti-seizure medication. This is all the normal routine.

I feel incredibly blessed with having a second chance in this journey through life. As our dear friend Mary Midla, Todd's wife, has always said, "There's no such thing as luck with God!" Instead of luck I use the word "blessed" when I speak or share words of encouragement. All my physicians, surgeons, techs, nurses, our friends and family are gifts from the Lord and most definitely play a role in this life-changing event in the journey. We're extremely grateful and immeasurably blessed!

CHAPTER | 24

It's Sunday and I'm Back Home

What a week we've had! We walk into our home for the first time since the surgery and it's super clean. My parents, siblings and Tom's side of the family and friends from our church have been taking care of the kids. We are so blessed! I thank my parents. Our kids run to greet us and all give me big bear hugs. I'm so happy to see them! I'm a survivor! Maybe I need to sign up for that TV show with Tom. After brain surgery I feel there's nothing I can't do.

Mom tells me how our church has a list of meals planned for us and how our neighbors also are bringing food over. My sister Teese comments on our church friends adding, "I've never met people like this. Are they real? It's like I've stepped into Pleasantville, literally. I wish I could take them back home to Florida with me."

I don't have to make dinner for a month! I'm overwhelmed by everyone's generosity. It's truly wonderful to know we are cared for and loved!

Not only is the house in order but I get another great surprise! As I'm sitting at the computer checking emails, I see a piece of paper on the desk. I read "Itinerary." What is this? It appears that either it's a continued joke about that Hawaii trip that Tom and Dr. Shapiro mentioned while I was in the hospital or is it for real? It looks like it's an official paper. It states Thomas and Kimberly Nguyen are booked on a flight to Honolulu, Hawaii for eight days. It's just for the two of us.

Well, after thinking it could be still a joke I go into the kitchen where Tom is standing and I quickly show him the itinerary. He smiles and says it's for real. I embrace Tom with a heartfelt hug and kiss him. I'm speechless once again! This speechlessness rarity does come at a price, but he did his homework and found a terrific deal! That's normally my department to find the deals, but I'm surely glad he was able to find this one. This is another "God thing!"

I never knew Tom could pull off such a big surprise. I'm impressed with his doing so. Not only has he planned for this adventure of a lifetime for us, but he has also planned where all the kids will go while we are away. Spencer and Rachel will stay with Mary and Todd, Calvin will be with Alex and Collin will stay with Ian. We really have great friends and family. I'm glad we are on "the family plan package deal!" I'm starting to sound like some sort of cell phone commercial from the television commercials. Ba Bomp! I still have my humor but not the tumor! Amen! Boy, am I glad I thought it was a joke when Dr. Shapiro mentioned it a few days ago because I am very pleasantly surprised!

CHAPTER | 25

Life After Surgery

JULY 19, 2003

I'm now at my third MRI since my surgery. The first one was on July 2nd for a brain mapping to prep me for surgery and the second one was on July 4th, the day after my surgery. But today I meet Dave, Christy and Jean, the ones operating the machine. They are very nice and bring a sense of comfort. My curiosity nags; I wonder how the surgery is healing. Did they get it all?

I take my shoes off, get more comfortable and lie on the MRI gurney. I hand my CD to Christy. I remembered to bring it so I could listen to good music. She hands it to Dave. I enjoy listening to contemporary Christian music. I tell Dave, "I want to listen to this instead of the jack hammer and the loud pounding noises of the MRI.

He smiles and says, "I can handle that for you. The scan will be a total of 30 minutes today. Christy will come in after the first 15 minutes and inject your veins with the dye contrast."

All of you who have been there and done that, with these scans performed, all of you know exactly what I'm talking about! It's just really, really loud. The needle doesn't scare me anymore.

Today Christy, Jean and Dave give me the comfort I need. I tell them, "I am a bit nervous about this particular scan. This is the defining moment from which I will get the news about whether the surgery took care of the tumor. They are checking for any residual tumor and also whether there has been any re-growth."

Christy taps my leg and says, "You'll do just fine."

The longer I lie on the gurney; the more I reminisce about all the many blessings I'm thankful for. There are so many! Christy and Jean are right at my side. Christy hands me the panic ball and says, "If you need to squeeze it, squeeze it and we'll be right here."

I say, "You know, I think I'll be just fine, but thank you." I still hold it in the palm of my right hand *just in case*.

Jean then asks, "Do you need a blanket?"

Since the room is chilly, I say, "Yes, thank you, Jean."

For this test I have to remain motionless. I wonder what happens if I have to sneeze? Now, Jean hands me the headphones so I can listen to the music. The other two times, I couldn't have headphones on because the scan required pinpoint accuracy for the surgery mapping. Therefore I know all about the jack hammer sounds. Moreover, it wouldn't work well because my tumor was on the right temporal lobe so close to my right ear. I'm thankful they allow me to have these headphones to partially mute the hammering.

Dave is ready to start the scan and does a sound check through the headphones. The music begins to play and I feel a need to sing so I do. My feet start to "dance." Maybe it's my nerves; I really don't know. But I know that during this scan I am not supposed to move, let alone tap my feet to music! All of a sudden Dave says, "Kim, is everything ok?

98

I say, "I'm doing fantastic!"

He says, "Kim I noticed movement on your scan and also see your feet are moving. I'm just checking to see if you are just trying to get my attention."

I reply, "No, I'm fine. I'm just in here dancing and praising the Lord for what he's done concerning the surgery."

He replies, "Ok, Kim, I'll turn your CD back on, but you must remain still for the remainder of the scan."

I reply, "Roger, over and out!" In these head phones it almost feels and sounds as though I might be in the cockpit of an airliner. Dave probably thinks I've lost my mind but I reassure him everything's all right. But, *technically speaking, perhaps I did lose some of my mind because Dr. Shapiro told me he had to take a little off around the edges of the brain around the bed of the tumor.* The music goes back on and I thank Dave.

"Praise the Lord. Sing to the Lord a new song...Let them praise His name with dancing..." (Psalm 149: 1-2).

After the second part of the scan when Christy injects the contrast dye into my veins, something happens. I have just prayed this scan will prove a successful surgery! "Lord I ask You to give me the peace and comfort of knowing it will all be just as You plan it." My heart is now pounding less. This is when something happens: following the prayer, I feel a hand grasp my left ankle and I feel such a peace. I think it must be Christy or Jean. Being the sweet and kind ladies they are, possibly one of them is giving me that tug for reassurance. After the scan I plan to ask them about it.

The scan has been in progress for 30 minutes and it is going much faster than I thought it would. I suppose the music helps pass the time more quickly. The gurney moves forward and I remain still just as I am told. Christy and Jean greet me with their beautiful smiles and I smile back. I ask Christy if it was she who gently placed her hand on my ankle. She looks at Jean and their answers surprises me! Christy says, "No, I didn't, and Jeans says, "It wasn't me."

I reply, "That's weird because about 15 minutes ago I said a prayer. I asked God for His peace and at that very moment I felt the warm embrace of a hand around my left ankle. I just figured it was one of you." I could sense they didn't know what to say and I, too, am speechless once again, but only for a moment. Again, they both say it wasn't they. As I leave, I tell my three friends that I'm a strong Christian and that God is truly my strength through this whole tumor situation.

I recall Jean saying, "Wow, Kim, we won't forget you and your faith!" Each give me a hug and Dave hands me the CD, saying he hopes the MRI wasn't too loud and I tell him, "It was just perfect." I can only sum this up as a "God thing."

CHAPTER | 26

Same Day – Follow Up Appointment with Dr. Dropcho

JULY 19, 2003

Now we head to the Indiana Cancer Center with my new pictures to learn the results we are all waiting for. I hold the answer in my hands. I am tempted to take a couple out and hold them up to the light to see if I can interpret what they show. But whom am I kidding? I wouldn't even know what to look for and I don't want to get any finger prints on them. I'm not a doctor but I might play one on TV if it's a production that involves Demi Moore and I'm her stunt double! Once again, humor minus the tumor! I need to control my curiosity; I will find out soon enough today what the results are.

Amazing: **1** *obsolete*: **BEWILDER, PERPLEX,** **2:** to fill with wonder: **ASTOUND** *intransitive verb*: to show or cause astonishment, **synonym** see SURPRISE

Source: *Merriam Webster Dictionary*

Something amazing happens as we get to the elevator on the first level of the Cancer Pavilion at Indiana University Medical Center. A blond lady approaches us and asks, "Are you looking for Dr. Dropcho's office?"

101

This catches me off guard and my mouth drops wide open. I say, "How did you know that?"

She replies, "The films you're holding kind of give it away."

I tell her, "Yes, as a matter of fact, we are heading to my appointment and we're uncertain where to go."

That's when she surprises us by saying, "Follow me, I'm his nurse. My name is Carolyn." I then introduce myself and Tom and we follow her. We're amazed at the coincidence, if it is only that.

She tells me to sign in and have a seat and she takes the folder of films and says the doctor will review them right away. Wow, she is actually my attending nurse! This is really amazing! I do sign in, but as I go to sit, I notice a picture collage hanging on the lobby wall. I get a closer look and it is Lance Armstrong. The headline reads "I'm alive because of Indiana University Hospital" and there are some other quotations from him on the magazine pages encased in the frame. This is more evidence that God is fully in control; no one knows this story better than I.

All these coincidences are not coincidences at all. They serve as a reminder to continue giving credit where it's due and to accept challenges and, most of all, to trust and know that God is who He says. Lance has slogans such as "Tour of Hope and Livestrong." I, too, have hope that I will continue this journey we call life. I plan to live a long time. I'm here for a reason.

> *For I know the plans I have for you declares the Lord, plans to prosper you and not to harm you, plans to give you **hope** and a future.*
>
> (Jeremiah 29:11, emphasis mine)

A nurse calls my name. Tom and I head to Dr. Dropcho to see what he thinks of the scan. He walks in and says, "Your scan shows some abnormalities with a darker image where the tumor was." He mentions something about possibly using chemo or radiation and proceeds to tell us the risks of and the differences between the two. Tom and I are still stuck on the word, "abnormalities." The doctor quickly adds, "The dark area can be a tumor re-growth or it can be scar tissue."

Being a believer and always hoping for the best, I boldly grab his forearm and say: "Dr. Dropcho, I'm going with the second one, scar tissue and I'm claiming that one in Jesus' name."

He is caught off guard and says, "Yes, that's quite possible." Because of these results, I'm told to come back for the next scan in about a month. The scheduled protocol for getting the scan every three months has now changed to getting it in one month.

Afterwards, I say to Nurse Carolyn, "I hope he wasn't offended by my saying that?"

She says, "I doubt it. He's a believer, too."

AUGUST 27, 2003

It's time for the follow-up scan to see if there has been any tumor re-growth. This time it is a different MRI tech named Steve. I hand him the Christian music CD and it's like déjà vu. It has only been a month. Because of that uncertain dark spot, they are keeping a close watch over me and I'm thankful. I really don't want to have to go through this again.

My headphones are given to me. This time I remain still, no dancing or singing. Dave may have given Steve a heads-up about what happened. I hear music and it brings peace. After the long 30 minutes, I get up and wait for the scans to be printed. Now we are going directly to my doctor's office as usual so he can give us the scan results today. No need for an escort this time around; we know where to go. Tom and I drop off the film early, so we head to the cafeteria. We have a nice lunch and nice time visiting. It's now time to head back to Dr. Dropcho's office for the results.

We sit for only a short time before my name is called. The front nurse, Jackie, takes note of this and later you will see what a role this episode plays. The doctor greets us and takes us to an examining room. We sit and he proceeds to tell us what the scan proved this time. He says, "Kim, your scan looks great! It doesn't show any change."

Tom and I take this as, "no tumor trying to grow." Amen! We're ecstatic and I blurt out: "Dr. Dropcho, do you recall during our previous visit, I claimed in Jesus' name that it was just scar tissue?"

He replies, "Yes, I do recall" *I really don't think he can ever forget that.*

I say, "Well, we are praising Him!"

After my appointment it's Jackie who had witnessed him coming to the lobby to get us who says, "Girl, I don't know what happened, but you had that man smiling and he normally doesn't smile. I mean, the man came out to get you personally."

I say, "Ms. Jones, maybe it's because I brought the Lord with me today!" I tell her of the good news that they think it's just scar tissue and she is happy for us as well.

CHAPTER | 27

Life at Home

Extraordinary; **1 a:** going beyond what is usual, regular, or customary <*extraordinary* powers> **b:** exceptional to a very marked extent -source: *Merriam Webster Dictionary*

I have another extraordinary experience. As I walk across the living room floor I hear an inner voice: "You were a farmer."

As God is my witness, and He most certainly is, I look up to the ceiling and say, "A farmer?"

Immediately I hear a reply. "You were a farmer in the hospital, sowing precious seeds for the Kingdom."

I reply, "Wow, Lord, I never thought of it like that. Thank you, Lord!"

Side note here: *I never farmed a day in my life until now.*

The door bell rings and to my surprise it's my sister-in-law, Mary Ann Mohney of Mohney Homes in Bloomington Indiana, bringing her friend to visit. Her friend just happens to be Priscilla, the first wife of Hoosier singer/song writer John Mellencamp. This is the first time she and I meet and what a lovely lady she is. God's beauty shines through her compassionate heart for me. God has the two of them here at His exact timing.

Priscilla presents a beautifully wrapped gift and says, "Kim, I wanted to bring you something and hope you will like it. After I showed it to Mary Ann she assured me you would like it and it will match your home décor." I thank her and begin to open it being careful as always when unwrapping presents. I finally have it unwrapped and the box open. I begin to cry because it is a bird bath inscribed with, *"His eye is on the sparrow, and I know He watches me."* She probably didn't expect me to cry and normally I don't cry over gifts, but her gift is another of those "God things" that keep happening.

You will recall the night before surgery when Tom, my sisters and I were singing and Teese said to Amy: "Amy, I think you have a song to sing… 'His Eye is on the Sparrow.'" And just moments before Mary Ann and Priscilla arrive; I have heard that I was a "farmer planting seeds for the Kingdom." Bird baths not only hold water but seeds, and this one happens to have that song we sang inscribed on the inside of it. Talk about coincidences! I don't think so!

I think maybe God is revealing this, because the tumor was meant to take place so others could see that, even in our lowest of valleys, we can have hope and trust that He is God. I read somewhere, "Without the valleys we can't appreciate the mountain tops." This is what it's all about; sharing our faith with others. We encounter storms in our life's journeys and there most certainly will be deep valleys, but He is always with us through it all and gives us the strength to carry on, regardless of the difficulty.

Where can I go from Your Spirit? Where can I flee from Your presence? If I go up to the heavens, You are there; if I made my bed in the depths, You are there. If I rise on the wings of the dawn, if I settle on the far side of the sea, even there Your hand will guide me; Your right hand will hold me fast.

(Psalm 139:7-9)

CHAPTER | 28

L to R: My sister Teese, Dr. Shapiro's wife, me, his mom, and Dr. Shapiro.

Tour of Hope

The Tour of Hope is a program for raising cancer awareness and trying to find a cure. It's a journey across America with 24 cyclists who are out to make a difference by raising awareness of the importance of cancer research and clinical trials. Lance Armstrong is the organization's spokesman.

OCTOBER 16, 2003

I can hardly believe time has traveled so fast. It's been three months since surgery. My hair is still pretty much shaved on the right side. I've been able to sport some really cute bandanas. It's great to have many bad hair days, because all I have to do is put on a bandana, tie it and voilà, I look great. I do wonder if my hair will ever grow back. Seems it's been a very slow process.

Today I plan to go downtown to Conseco Field House to attend the Tour of Hope. My sister-in-law, Kim, was given the tickets and she chose to give them to us. We both share the same name, Kim Nguyen. She is the assistant dean of the school of science at Indiana University Purdue University in Indianapolis. She knows I'm the one who will benefit most from attending the function.

It's a program designed to help raise awareness of cancer research and the importance of clinical trials. World Cyclist Champion Lance Armstrong is the keynote speaker. As mentioned earlier, Lance and I share the same superior neurosurgeon, Dr. Scott Shapiro, and this is why Kim thinks of giving me the tickets.

Tom is unable to go, so I ask my sister Teese to take his place. I tell her I think my doctor will be there and I want to get more details from him for the book. You will recall she lives in Florida. She has flown up to stay and is nursing me during my recovery.

We arrive at Conseco in plenty of time for the program. I notice the parking lot is mostly filled with mini vans. We park and head to the elevator. As we go into the elevator, a blond lady is standing with tickets in her shirt pocket. No, it's not my blond nurse, Carolyn. That would be strange! I notice her tickets are a different color from ours. Being like our dad and having never met a stranger, I speak to her first: I say, "I see we are going to the same place, but your tickets are a different color."

She says, "My husband is a testicular cancer survivor and we are sitting in the survivor section."

I then quickly turn my partially shaved head and show her the question mark scar. I say, "I too, am a survivor. I had a brain tumor removed three months ago."

Teese adds, "It was the size of a baseball."

The blond lady seems surprised that I'm doing so well. I tell her, "By the way, I'm Kim and this is my sister Teese."

She replies, "Hi, I'm Mickey."

Then she congratulates me and asks what my symptoms were and how the tumor was discovered. My response: "I had headaches for 20-some days and then was hit in the head by a golf ball. It hurt like blazes and I decided to get an examination. It's really a 'God thing' that I'm still here. Trust me. It's such a story that I'm currently writing a book about it."

She is amazed and says, "Wow, a golf ball, good thing you were there at the right place and time to get hit!"

"Yes, it's a blessing!"

She replies, "I'm proud of you. Keep writing; it sounds like your story will encourage who need it." Could Mickey be someone God sent to cross paths with us today? It surely seems that way.

As we leave the elevator, I tell Teese, "I feel we need to stick near her."

She then jokingly says, "We don't want her to think we are stalking her!"

I ask, "Mickey, would it be alright if we stick by you and your husband?"

She replies, "It's totally fine with me, but I'm not sure you will be able to without the same color ticket."

I tell her, "I'm not worried about that. I'll just show the ticket clerks that I, too, am a survivor and we'll be admitted." *I've been told numerous times that I'm a very determined person and I am.*

As we approach the ticket lady, I say, "I'm a survivor; may we sit in the survivor section?"

She replies, "Absolutely, I don't see why not. I'm so happy for you to have made it here today."

I reply, "Thank you. The Lord has done some great work on me."

As Teese and I sit down, it is as if we are sitting in a great sea of miracles! It is so comforting to know that each of us is still here for some purpose. We feel as though we are in the river mentioned in Ezekiel 47:3-4: ankle deep, knee deep, waist deep and deep enough to swim in. *"Swarms of living creature will live wherever the river flows"* (Ezekiel 47:9). Wherever the river is, there is life. Spared life is all around us!

Prior to the start of the program, I remind her that, "I'm **confident** we will see my doctor here today and I will be able to talk with him and get more details for the book."

Teese replies, "Baby, he's a very busy man. I don't know whether you will see him today or not."

I reply, "Oh, we will!" Lance Armstrong walks to the podium and the program begins.

It's now toward the end of the program and Teese spots someone. She says, "Kimmie, I think that's your doctor!"

I look where she is pointing and say, "That's he." She doesn't have the best of eyesight but I'm glad she was able to spot him in this large arena and crowd of at least 5000 to 6000 people. He is on the front row, ground level. I say to her, "He was Lance's brain surgeon. He should be up on stage with the other doctors who are being recognized! Lance is up there talking and walking and he is cycling because of Dr. Shapiro's beautiful work."

I tell her, "I want to go say hi to him after the program."

She says, "We are gonna' be like salmon swimming up stream with all these people here."

I remind her I need to get more details. She says, "All right, let's go." Even my sister knows I'm too determined to be swayed. We begin to walk down the bleacher "against the tide." Actually, the crowd doesn't slow us even though we are "swimming upstream." Imagine that!

I see that Dr. Shapiro is engaged in conversation as we wait a mere 20 feet away. When he finishes his conversation, he looks our direction and our eyes meet. He says, "Well, hello Kim!"

I reply, "Dr. Shapiro, you remember me?"

He says, "Of course I do. I never forget any of my patients."

I reply, "I'll bet you remember my talking about the Lord."

He says, "No, now that's not why." We all smile. I introduce Teese and he says, "Yes, I remember you from the hospital. It's so nice to see you again," and they shook hands.

He smiles and says, "Kiddo, I'm so glad you're doing so well!"

I say, "Dr. Shapiro, remember in the hospital when I told you I was going to write a book?"

He replies, "Yes, I do remember your telling me that."

I say, "Well, I'm currently working on my manuscript and I'm here today in hopes of getting more details from you."

He replies, "That's wonderful. Keep it up!" He then turns to his left and says, "Kiddo, this is my mother. Mom, this is Kim Nguyen,

113

she is one of my former patients from a couple months ago."

I say, "July 3rd."

He smiles and says, "She remembers."

Dr. Shapiro stands to my right and his mother to my left and I say, "Mrs. Shapiro, I'm so honored to meet you. I thank God for creating in you this wonderful man." I say this while taking my right thumb and motioning it over my right shoulder to where he stands.

She smiles and says, "He's a keeper." We are all smiling and I feel that meeting his mom is another "God thing." I mean, how in the world would I have ever got the opportunity otherwise?!

While standing between Dr. Shapiro and his mother, I feel the urge to tell him *now* about the operating room event. I say, "Dr. Shapiro, I have something I need to tell you about the surgery day. It's a 'God thing,' so may I tell you?"

He replies, "Yes, please." So, I then tell him the news that God was using his hands and eyes as His instruments, but He was the One performing the operation. I told him I heard this while on the OR surgery bed prior to Dr. Keever's even coming into the OR to give me the knock-out meds.

I quickly ask, "Do you believe me?"

He replies, "Yes, I do and thank you very much for sharing it with me."

Having heard what I just said, his mom says, "Kim that's wonderful! You've been given a second chance, now do something with it."

I say, "I am. I'm writing about this journey with God through my trials."

She replies, "I can't wait to read it. Please be sure to get me a copy."

I tell her, "Don't you worry, I shall. It's because of the Lord's using your son's hands and eyes as His instruments for my surgery that I'm alive and well today." We embrace in a most definite heart-felt hug.

I say to Dr. Shapiro, "Oh yeah, I want to let you know something else. You didn't blow the Hawaii surprise. Tom did book the flight for this November and I was still surprised because I just thought you were joking around. Now I know that Tom was up to something during my first appointment with you. He had asked you if the metal plates and screws from my surgery would set off airport metal detectors."

He replies, "Yes, he was concerned because he wanted to take you on this trip. He asked if you could make the trip and I told him it would be fine to take you to Hawaii!" I thank him for approving the excursion. While smiling, he replies, "Guess you won't have to wait until Heaven to go, as you told me in the hospital. I'm glad for you. You both will enjoy it!"

Then Dr. Shapiro's wife finished her conversation with others and his mom said to the younger Mrs. Shapiro, "This is Kim Nguyen, one of Scott's former patients." Her eyes opened widely. She paused, looked at her husband and back at me and pointed with her right index finger saying, "Scott, is this the one?"

He smiles back at her and while nodding his head says, "Yes, she's the one!" She then embraced me for what seemed a whole minute and I embrace her with that same passion.

During the hug she says, "I'm so glad to meet you, Kim."

115

Now, what did she mean when she paused and asked, "Scott, is this the one?" I sense that she may have heard of my good attitude and how I was always positive despite the seriousness of the surgery. Maybe he told her how calm I was going into surgery with the 104/60 blood pressure and the 100% oxygen level! I think he suspected during surgery he and Dr. Miller weren't the only ones who were performing it. Maybe he knew he had an extra set of hands guiding his own to remove my mass and he shared that with her? He knew exactly how calm I was when I received the news of the tumor and also that I was calm up to the time of surgery. And I'm sure he remembers my telling him I was actually looking forward to my surgery.

Maybe my nurses told him about my faith in the Lord and how I was confident that God handpicked him for my surgery! Maybe this is the reason for young Mrs. Shapiro's comment to him. Just the fact that she knows my name means something special. The Lord knows exactly what it all means.

We have enjoyed our time together. I am thankful that we all met today: Mrs. Shapiro, Dr. Shapiro and his beautiful wife. I'm grateful for the words of encouragement each has shared with me. I have even gotten the material I need for the book. I pray for its publication and for you and all the others reading about my sublime journey. The Lord is faithful and I'm grateful.

We are all special to God so I believe my case is a routine "God thing." I'm just a sinner saved by God's amazing grace. But I'm sure it is my destiny to share my story with you. I'm not a preacher, but God has given me a story to live and tell.

> *With man this is impossible, but not with God; all things are possible with God.*
>
> (Mark 10:27)

CHAPTER | 29

Hawaii November/December 2003

MORE SURPRISES!

The flight is long but I know what awaits us in those delightful islands, beauty galore! I've seen the pictures in travel magazines, but can the place really be so beautiful? We are about to find out.

We have now landed and are taxiing on the runway at Honolulu International Airport. Just up the ramp we see a couple of familiar faces and a guy holding a hand-made sign that reads, "Nguyen."

They are dressed in Hawaiian style, including the leis around their necks. It is none other than our dear friends from church, Wendell and Susanne! The joke is on me and once again I'm speechless. Hey, maybe that's why Tom is doing all of this, so I won't talk so much? I'm starting to feel as though I'm being video-taped for some "Got Ya!" TV show! I look around but see no cameras, not even Demi Moore.

I hug Tom and tell him, "You are something! Thank you, Hon!" We run and I hug them; Wendell places a beautiful lei' around my neck. Susanne places a masculine one around Tom's neck. I've only seen this happen in the movies!

Next I look around to see if Don Ho is around. We are all smiles and I say, "Wow, Tom really pulled a big one on me!" I echo the words of Dr. Shapiro's mother at Conseco Field House: "He's a keeper!" Our friends tell me that Tom's had this planned since the surgery and it worked out perfectly because they are in Hawaii to spend family time with Wendell's parents here. Wendell grew up in Hawaii. Susanne just happens to be pregnant with their first child. They are planning a family celebration of their soon-to-be baby; there will be a big baby shower with their family. What a great day filled with continual surprises! Little do I know what to expect for the rest of the trip?

Our church friends are our personal tour guides for the island. We get to the hotel and unpack. We have a two bedroom so we can all be together. The next morning first thing before the sun rises we head out to the ocean. We actually walk to the beach and have a breakfast buffet. It's at a fantastic hotel located right on the ocean front. We get there just before the sun rises. Wow!!! What a sight!!!! It's most breathtaking. I've never seen anything more beautiful! The weather couldn't be kinder.

118

The view is priceless and the food is irresistible. I can hardly wait to try the vast variety of foods! I wish we had plants like this in our yards back home in Indiana. Stunning birds are flying and the waves are tossing back and forth gently. This is reality at its finest!

I can't resist putting a bit of pineapple on my plate from the buffet. It's absolutely luscious! It is the sweetest, juiciest, and indeed best I've ever eaten. All the other foods are wonderful as well. I tell Tom I think we can live here, I could get used to all of this! He and I smile. We are holding hands like newlyweds.

Later, we do some sightseeing and I'm amazed that Hawaii is even more beautiful in person than any portrayal I've ever seen or heard. We are on the freeway; it has just rained briefly and out of nowhere we see an astonishing thing, a *double* rainbow. I've never seen this kind of thing before! Even the flowers seem as though they are out of this world. It's the richness of their colors. If this is earth, I can't wait to see what's in Heaven! Hawaii is magnificent.

On the second morning, Wendell prepares a wonderful breakfast for us. He is an excellent cook just as Tom is. The two of them enjoy cooking. I'm the baker in the family. It works out great! Really, I enjoy cooking gourmet meals, too, at home. But we are on vacation! This is great! We actually have our own chef, too. Wendell and Susanne are most hospitable!

Wendell prepares a wonderful breakfast including fresh fruit and guava jelly on this scrumptious sweet Hawaiian bread. I'll exercise it all off when we get home. But for now, we are on vacation. I plan to try all the different dishes and all the fresh fruit I can lay my hands on. The pineapple just knocked my socks off. Oh, I'm wearing sandals.

I can hardly wait to see where we will be venturing next. Our friends are going to take us to some restaurants favored by the locals. I would guess that most tourists don't have personal tour guides who were born and raised in Hawaii and know where all the great hideaways are. Ah, but we do! Wendell tells us he will take us to see some waterfalls in the mountains that are really beautiful and hard to find. He says some movie scenes were shot there for the movie Jurassic Park. I'm grateful that we have such excellent guides. We are truly blessed with this awesome experience with great friends! I'm taking beautiful pictures which will augment the great memories we will have of this vacation.

We venture to a local place for lunch. To outsiders it looks like "a hole in the wall." But sometimes back home restaurants like these turn out to be pretty good. On our own, we'd never have found this place. We walk in and smell great food. We seat ourselves and look over the menus. The beauty of having our friends with us is we just ask them what to order and they know exactly. They tell us they find this place to be most authentic of all the Hawaiian restaurants on the island of Oahu, and the prices are reasonable. I am amazed at how inexpensively we can actually eat here. I was always told it's so expensive to eat in Hawaii. Well, not when you have your personal tour guides escorting you away from the pricey tourist areas.

We order many of the recommended dishes, one being Kalua pig. While waiting for the food to arrive, we have great conversation. It's a wonderful vacation in this Pacific paradise; just the four of us enjoying adult conversation. I do miss the kids though! We all like this Kalua pig dish. It's like a barbeque the likes of which few outside Hawaii have tasted.

For an extra treat after dinner Wendell, takes us to his favorite shaved ice place. It's well known by the locals and they really do have great ice cream and shaved ice. What a treat!

Next is another adventure but Susanne is skipping this one because she is pregnant and says she will rest. Wendell drives us to the Honolulu International Airport. This puzzles me. On the other side of the airport is a smaller airfield and this is where the surprise begins. He seems to know most of the guys. This doesn't surprise us because he is an airline transport pilot for a major airline company in Indy. We walk up to a smaller blue and white airplane. Wendell says, "This is a Cessna 172." I'm now thinking he's giving us an airfield tour. This is pretty cool! He tells us to have a seat and we do. He gets in the cockpit and tells us to buckle up and put on the head phones. He now informs us that he has rented this Cessna airplane and is taking us for a personal tour by air today.

I have the still and video cameras in my tote. Wendell shows us by air where parts of the Jurassic Park movie were filmed. I can see why, because it is wide open fields in mountain ranges and absolutely gorgeous. Even though we saw it from the drive the other day it is most magnificent by air. It almost seems as though we were making some kind of documentary. This seems so unreal – much like the news of the trip. But what a blast we are having! We have the blessing of great friends.

We see the mountain tops and the valleys which remind me of what we've been through recently as a family. Without the valleys we can't appreciate the mountain tops. It's absolutely pristine. There are gigantic waterfalls among these huge mountains. We flew completely around the island of Oahu, where we saw the North Shore and many other areas of interest.

We have no idea about the extent of their plans for this private plane trip; what a grand surprise! Our friends are good at keeping poker faces because this turns out to be a great adventure.

Side note: Susanne will inform us after we return that she was well aware of the private flight Wendell had planned. Her thought was she'd put us over the weight limit, being pregnant; thus the reason she decided to "stay and rest." She too has a long career in the airline industry. She is a flight attendant and has been for many years.

During our vacation we are also able to attend a concert at a local shopping mall. It's Christmas time with all the red and green décor in the mall. There must be thousands of poinsettias making up this gorgeous Christmas tree in the center of the mall. The concert is performed here. It is a very rare occasion because the concert is free and it presents none other than the most popular group in Hawaii, Na Leo. Their voices are quite angelic; one sounds like Karen Carpenter. We just happen to be here at the right time and right place.

It reminds me somewhat of being at the right place another time, the time of that fateful golf ball. Hmmm. It's one more "God thing." God continues to amaze us with all the blessings He continues to bestow upon us.

122

We actually meet the performers personally after the concert and we buy several of their CD's. We also buy the video entitled "*Na Leo Pilimehana Christmas Is Giving.*" On the back cover, we read, "Christmas is always a joyous time of year, but here in Hawaii, Christmas is somehow even more magical." I agree. These talented musicians are so kind and real. They make time to take pictures with us as well as sign a few of the CD's for our daughter Rachel. She will be just thrilled when we take this music back home to her.

One of the singers actually gives me her beautifully fragranced lei' as she welcomes us to her home state of Hawaii. Susanne tells me afterward that it is quite an honor for the singer to give me these flowers; these particular flowers are the most expensive from which leis are made. This is almost too good to be true!

During one of our adventures we go to an actual luau. This luau is held at the Polynesian Cultural Center and, according to our guides, is one of the best. There are many famous popular Hawaiian singers here. The food is fantastic. Our table is about 100 to 150 feet from the stage. But, during the show, the performers pick members of the audience to teach how to dance Hawaiian style. I am one of the impromptu students. There are a total of maybe ten of us who are invited to come down on stage and learn to dance in front of the audience of well over 1000. The announcer who is doing the choosing looks in our direction and says, "You, the lady with the lei on your head."

I look around and Susanne is quick to say, "Kim I think he means you." Maybe I'm the only one brave enough to actually wear it on my head, but the person who sold it to me said this one is for that purpose. We four are all smiles and Susanne says something like, "Only with Kim can we have such adventure."

I venture down toward the stage with some embarrassment because I'm not a good dancer. Ah, but the beauty of it is in all the fun we are having. Oh well, this crowd will never see me again and it's ok if I make fool of myself up here. Perhaps the other nine will, too. This vacation continues to be a "God thing!" We are having a blast. Our time here together is like dating all over again with a second honeymoon for good measure.

Next, we are on a shopping adventure. We are purchasing a lot of trinkets: lots of nick knacks such as leis and jewelry. We even buy island-fresh macadamia nuts in a place most tourists would never find. This shopping comes once a year and is hosted in a big sports arena. I'm telling you we would have never known of all the goodies for sale here without our friend's help. And the prices are quite reasonable. It's like a giant market with many quality goods for sale. There are many fruits, different coffees and a variety of plants available for purchase. There are island clothes galore to bring back as keepsakes. Tom is searching for more guava fruit, but, so far, finds none. He speaks of possibly finding some in the wild on our adventures.

Next our adventure is a visit to the Dole Pineapple Plantation. We take a train ride through the park to see all the different kinds of pineapples. The song playing over the speakers as we travel is performed by none other than Na Leo, the group we enjoyed at the concert. It is quite popular with Hawaiians. Next, we take the scenic walking tour and find a sign that states the pineapples in this part of the plantations are Vietnamese. I take Tom's picture in front of it as a keepsake. We buy a couple of pineapples and take them back to our hotel where Tom carves them up later as a late night treat.

We also go to North Shore. This is where big-time surfers perform. The waves are supposed to be the best in the world. People come from everywhere to surf the waves here. Today happens to be a day that ESPN Sports are here videotaping famous and local surfers. The waves are huge. I remember seeing this area when Wendell announced over the headphones in the Cessna, "We are now approaching the North Shore, home of many big surf competitions. We will visit it again on foot later this week to see surfing at its best!"

While at North Shore later on we do observe surfing at its best. Many pros pass by us heading out to the sea to catch waves. Most of the surfers have bleached blond hair. I'm almost certain it must be sun-bleached hair rather than from a bottle. This weather is awesome and the sun is incredible. One surfer comes up from a big crash and is walking past us with his board which is literally broken in two. That had to have hurt! These are serious surfers. They are filming something about Extreme Sports for ESPN. What a terrific week we are having here on the islands! We couldn't have asked for a greater vacation, so fun-filled and packed with memories of great food and fellowship.

Another adventure later this week happens at Hanauma Bay, a public beach. Wendell and Susanne say this is the best place to go snorkeling on Oahu because of the reef that protects the bay, keeps the water calm and attracts lots of fish. It's not very crowded either. I may actually get a tan here in Hawaii! The locals know about this place and it's popular with tourists too, but some people just don't make the effort to go out of Waikiki. Waikiki beach isn't the greatest, but it's only a few blocks away from any hotel.

To us Hanauma Bay is a great hideaway that our friends share. The turtles are the largest I've ever seen. It looks as though I could ride on one of them but I pass on that. We put on our snorkeling gear and for the first time in my life I get to view the sea life that movie character Dori saw in the movie "Finding Nemo." She had a loss of memory just as I did prior to the tumor diagnosis.

It's a whole new world down here below the surface. It's fabulous! Wendell and Susanne say that Tom fits in like a local. "You guys could move the family down here. What do you think?"

We say, "That would be great!"

During each evening we take a stroll down the main drag and there are so many singers at hotels that dazzle guests with beautiful Hawaiian music. This place is so relaxing that I could get used to it.

After another concert outdoors we encounter a man named Zen who does charcoal portraits of people. I tell Tom I'd like him to do one of us. We wait our turn and he does such a beautiful job that we later frame it. Tom asks him if he would give me normal hair. We explain that I just had brain surgery which accounts for the temporary sparseness. He did fill it in quite nicely. He gives us his address and tells us he is a professor of art at a prominent university here.

This is another day and, as we drive from our hotel, Tom spots a beautiful guava tree. He is from Vietnam and misses the tropical fruits with which he grew up. Wendell stops the car near the tree. Susanne and I are laughing. This is so much fun! Tom and Wendell are outside the car doing their best to knock fruit off the tree. Tom is very determined. Presently, the men do shake loose some of the luscious fruit. One is ripe. I video tape the action; maybe one day I'll submit it to America's Funniest Videos – might even win some prize money. As our husbands get closer to the car, I noticed Tom carries the guava with gentleness.

Side note: This reminds me of the character Frodo Baggins in the movie "Lord of the Rings." The scene that comes to my mind is when

126

he is wearing the ring around his neck on a necklace and addresses it as, "My Precious." Now don't get me wrong, Tom wasn't playing the role to a tee. He was holding the guava very tenderly, that's all. Later, back at our hotel, he washes and cuts his treasure. I can say that it is the most fantastic fruit I've ever tasted. It has a pink "flesh" inside and is quite sweet.

This week we participate in a very special day in our friends' lives. I'm grateful that God has blessed Wendell and Susanne with a child for which they have yearned for so long. We have the honor of attending Susanne's first baby shower. It is held at Wendell's parents' house in Kahalu'u. We meet his siblings and aunts and uncles and cousins. This is quite a reunion! They know how to throw a party Hawaiian style. I even learn some of the language. They laugh as I attempt to speak the words I've just been taught by the aunts and cousins. It's fun!

Prior to the baby shower, Wendell shows Tom some of the different fruit plants and fruit trees in his parents' yard. The grapefruits are huge. This is paradise for Tom. Wish we could have plants and trees like these back home in Indiana.

Wendell points to a tree on the small hill next to his parents' house and says, **"Tom, look there's a guava**. There's only one. Do you want to climb up and get it?" Of course Tom is game and does it.

Side note: After we return home to Indiana, it becomes a common joke for Wendell to blurt out, "Tom, look there's a guava." Tom looks every time with a genuine smile on his face. The other three of us smile, too.

On our last full day in Hawaii, Tom treats us to the best local restaurant. This fancy restaurant is called Sam Choy's Breakfast,

Lunch and Crab. It is where the locals go for dinner. The place is packed and there are many on the waiting list. We are fortunate to have a table. This is where Tom eats a dish called "poke." It consists of raw seafood cut into cubes and dressed with sauces and spices. Tom becomes hooked on it. I want him to enjoy it all, so I pass on tasting it. I'm glad he and Wendell love the dish.

We had a magnificent time the entire stay. We hope that one day we can afford to bring the whole family with us. Wendell's parents have invited us to come back and visit with them.

This is so much fun. We truly would have never been able to find all these places on our own. And we wouldn't be able to try without our friends and family who are taking care of our kids back in Indiana. They are such a blessing! Blessings just keep coming in many ways, including health, friends, food and great times. We are blessed by our friendship as brothers and sisters in Christ. We are so grateful.

This is a magnificent place on earth and compares with no other place I've been, with an incredible amount of splendor. I'm thankful to be able to enjoy the beauty of His creation! Thank You, Lord, for allowing me to go on living. And this experience is "really living."

The heavens declare the glory of God; the skies proclaim the work of His hands.

(Psalm 19:1)

CHAPTER | 30

First Mother's Day
After Surgery

MAY 13, 2004, 5:45 A.M.

Today is Mother's Day and I'm so grateful I've survived to celebrate it! As I sit on my whitewashed wicker arm chair, I'm in awe.
I am blessed with life to celebrate this special day with my wonderful husband and all my wonderful children. Today the weather is
perfect; the breeze couldn't be any kinder. I listen to the birds as they
chirp their lovely melodies; I've never noticed just how lovely they

sound until now. As I sit here and look at the bird bath Priscilla gave me, I smile. Remember, it's inscribed "Your promise Lord." He even cares about the sparrow's welfare. He is watching as I enjoy His creation. He continues to watch over me since my surgeries!

I thank the Lord for our senses of hearing, sight, touch, smell and taste: they enable us to know of His wonderful creations. My baseball-sized brain tumor was diagnosed just nine months ago, but now life is being revealed magnificently. Nine months to give life in baby form and nine months to give life in the form of deliverance from that dark valley of the tumor. Almost like a new birth because I have a greater appreciation for life and I've been given a second chance! I notice the little things. Even the air has a fresher perfume; all the flowers and pines around me have a fragrance that no processed perfume could even approach.

> *Consider it pure joy, my brothers, whenever you face trials of many kinds, because you know that the testing of your faith develops perseverance. Perseverance must finish its work so that you may be mature and complete, not lacking anything. If any of you lacks wisdom, he should ask God, who gives generously to all without finding fault, and it will be given to him. But when he asks, he must believe and not doubt, because he who doubts is like a wave of the sea, blown and tossed by the wind. That man should not think he will receive anything from the Lord; he is a double minded man, unstable in all he does.*
>
> (James 1:2-5)

> *Blessed is the man who perseveres under trial, because when he has stood the test, he will receive the crown of life that God has promised to those who love him.*
>
> (James 1:12)

I know through my trials, He is making me stronger in terms of my physical health and my faith. I continue to pray for His strength because according to Dr. Shapiro, this type of tumor has a tendency to be followed by another. I will continue to trust and to keep my faith that God is ultimately in control no matter what happens!

Just as the birds continue to whistle and chirp, I want to continue telling the good news of all He's done and continues to do in my life and the promise that He will never leave or forsake any of us. My prayer for this book is that others may find God if they are searching.

For those who are believers and may have gone astray, I pray your faith will be strengthened as mine most definitely has been. I find that it's a daily walk with Him. My prayer is that you can experience the peace that can't be explained, and a strength that can't be diminished even when life gets tough and we get curveballs thrown at us. It's a continuous journey. With firsthand knowledge, I testify boldly to the truth of these verses that have motivated this book:

> *I can do all things through Him who gives me strength.*
> (Philippians 4:13)

> *Even though I walk through the valley of the shadow of death, I will fear no evil, for You are with me; Your rod and Your staff, they comfort me.*
> (Psalm 23:4)

CHAPTER | 31

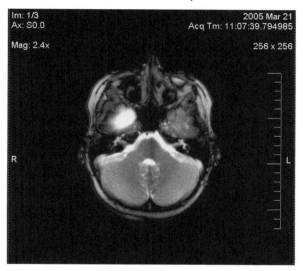

Im: 1/3
Ax: S0.0
2005 Mar 21
Acq Tm: 11:07:39.794985
Mag: 2.4x
256 x 256
R
L

I Have Another Tumor?

FEBRUARY 7, 2005 & MARCH 21, 2005 MRI SCANS

I continue to have MRIs of my brain as ordered every three months. And all is well so far. At today's appointment, Dr. Dropcho tells me there is some "thickening of the rim" in the bed of where the tumor once was.

I will get another MRI on March 21, 2005 to see if there have been any changes. I'm told to see Dr. Shapiro and I do.

On this March 21st appointment with Dr. Shapiro, he tells me, "I think I'll be able to go in and get it with no problems."

I say, "Excuse me? Go in and get what, Dr. Shapiro?"

"Well, Hon, you have another brain tumor!" Needless to say, I am shocked! I suppose this is a moment of disbelief because I can't even cry.

I ask him, "How can this be? Dr. Dropcho never mentioned it to me; just something about some thickening of the rim and that maybe it's scar tissue?"

But Dr. Shapiro replies, "Sorry to be the bearer of this news. I'm just blunt." At this point I ask if he will show me the x-rays and he escorts me into the room where they hang on the white lighted board. While pointing to the scan, he says, "Here it is in October 2004 and it's still present today (March 21, 2005.)" It has only been 19 months since my first tumor and now another craniotomy is needed. Wow! He tells me he'll be able to use the same entrance at the now-healed scar. He says, "Don't worry, you'll still be gorgeous."

I reply, "I like that part of your bluntness!" Humor, despite a second brain tumor: I do believe laughter is good medicine when a brain tumor is diagnosed.

It's really in how one looks at the circumstances. We all have choices; do we become bitter and disenchanted? Or do we look at a problem with a different perspective and say, "This must be how it's meant to be. What is God trying to teach me from this?" For me, I believe it was meant to create a new love and appreciation for life and to have a closer relationship with the Creator. Is this second tumor one more test of my faith? Well, if it is a test, I expect to ace it.

134

It was only five days before those mysterious and fateful headaches in 2003 that I had prayed for Him to relight my fire as it had once burned when I was a faithful Christian. My life as a Christian had grown stagnant then and I felt that I was missing something. Well, He lit me up again big time; a bonfire with marshmallows, graham crackers and a chocolate bar again! I attest to the fact that God has a way of getting us to our knees if we are willing to take the necessary action. Believe me, it's a good place to be!

Pam McCracken, Dr. Shapiro's assistant and second hand, sets my surgery date for March 31, 2005. I guess I can be devastated or I can go at this with confidence that it will be taken care of. The only good thing about getting a craniotomy twice is I am well schooled in this field. The medical people will glue fiducials on my head for the brain mapping, then anesthetics will be injected into my veins; the hair on the right side has to be shaved again (just when I have started to like my new do). They'll surgically produce a cranial flap (the question mark incision) in order to get to my brain, cut a piece of my skull out, drill burr holes and then operate with precision, including the use of a microscope. After that, they will place the skull piece back into my puzzle with titanium screws and plates and so much more. I'm well schooled in all this now. Perhaps I can be Pam's office assistant if they ever have an employment opportunity.

MARCH 29, 2005

I may look like Frankenstein for a couple of days since surgery is only two days away, but it's ok. It gives me the opportunity to share, when people ask me why I have these metal dots all over my head. Cheryl strategically glued the dots (fiducials) for my first surgery and she is doing it again for the second. The fact is she makes me feel comfortable. See how I'm looking at this bad situation in a good way? I could be thinking negatively but why should I? God has it all in His control and I'm thankful. "The Lord is my shepherd" and I shall not be lost. I have His strength and hope for a future, it will carry me through. I'm quite confident.

May Your unfailing love rest upon us, O Lord, even as we put our hope in You.

(Psalm 33:22)

As for God, His way is perfect...For who is God besides the Lord? And who is the Rock except our God? It is God who arms me with strength and makes my way perfect.

(2 Samuel 22:31-33)

Webster's Thesaurus: Rock: "Firm or solid, defense, support, Rock of Gibraltar; see foundation.

Strength: Sturdiness, fortify, reinforce, confirm, encourage, increase, multiply, empower, sustain."

MARCH 30, 2005

My husband, children, Tom's older brother, Tom, and his wife, Kim, (the ones who gave us the Tour of Hope tickets – yes, there are two Tom's and Kim's), my younger sister, Amy, our friends Todd and Mary Midla and I all go to our favorite Vietnamese restaurant this night for the last big meal before my big surgery. I am told not to eat after midnight so I take it literally since it's only 6 p.m. Yes, I do get lots of stares but it's alright.

My quote:
"I find it ironic that it took a golf ball hit to my head to find the first tumor (size of a baseball) and now the second tumor is the size of a golfball. It's not another coincidence, no way!"

136

CHAPTER | 32

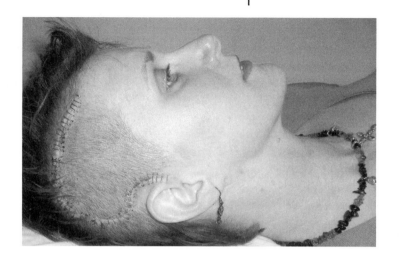

Second Surgery

MARCH 31, 2005, 6 A.M.

I get to visit with my family and friends from our church. It is a little bit different from the first surgery since surgery time is scheduled at 6:30 a.m., whereas it took place in the early afternoon the first time on July 3, 2003. Today we don't have as much time to visit and play. It's time to prep for surgery so I head to get my gown. As I leave, I say, "Bye. I'll be back soon and I hope to get a better hair cut this time." Everyone laughs and I leave on a happy note because laughter helps once again.

I don't have the same anesthesiologist this time. Now it's Dr. Rosenfeld; his is the same name as my dentist's. Dr. Rosenfeld is very nice and quite jovial, just as my other physicians are. I'm in perfect harmony with all the skilled hands of the physicians and the comforting nurses whom God chose by hand for me. I feel God's presence; I'm not going through this valley alone. *Having a good attitude despite the circumstance you may be in is a key element. It's all in how one looks at her or his situation; looking at it in a positive way is most healthful.*

I am now lying on the operating room bed. A nurse comes to my side, hands me a phone and tells me I have a phone call. All right, is this some kind of joke? Just minutes before Dr. Rosenfeld injects me with the anesthetics, I'm taking a phone call? This is crazy. I find it strange, but I smile and answer, "Hello, I'm kind of busy at the moment. What do you need?"

The voice is that of my sister, Amy. She just wants me to know that she loves me and to know that I'm being prayed for. She says that my loved ones were disappointed that they couldn't spend as much time with me as they did the first time. I tell her, "Thank you, Sis. I will be all right though, just as before. I love you, too, and you know it!" She hands the phone to our other sister, Teese, aka Terri, and she echoes the sentiment. Next, it is our pastor, Jim Burks. He wants to pray with me and he does. He prays that God will guide Dr. Shapiro and Dr. Sloan's hands during the surgery according to His will for my life. He tells me they will be praying in the waiting area during surgery as well.

I thank him and say, "I'm surely loved. It really means a lot. They need me for the surgery now so I'll talk with you guys later." Focusing on the phone call, I forget that they are injecting my veins. I hand the phone back to the nurse and I drift from consciousness. I don't remember a thing, just as was the case with Dori, the "Nemo" movie fish. Yep, won't remember a thing.

I'm glad they let me accept the call. It emphasized the love of my family and friends and that they are sending prayers up on my behalf. I know God is with me to endure one more hardship.

Let me backtrack a little bit. Just prior to this morning's surgery, Dr. Shapiro had told my family and friends that the operation would last about six hours, same as the time before. So everyone was visiting and reminiscing about the first surgery. Tom's sister went to get egg rolls and other Vietnamese finger foods during the first surgery...Tom is the one to make the food run for everyone this time.

However, when he returns today he is told my surgery is completed. He is floored that surgery went that quickly. It went better than was anticipated and took less time. My mom, Peggy, recalls Dr. Shapiro's comment, "Surgery went smooth as silk!" She shares that comment with me, but I have heard him as well.

Just as with the first surgery, I say, "Silk is pretty smooth!"

He replies once again, "Yes, it went that smoothly, Kiddo."

Great news, it's all over now and a success. ***But*** there is another curve to this ball; the pathologist discovers a problem. My tumor is classified as mixed oligoastrocytoma anaplastic, WHO (World Health Organization) grade III. It is located on the right temporal/frontal lobe this time. The first time the tumor was classified as an oligodendroglioma astrocytoma low grade benign (non-cancerous), located on the right temporal lobe only. In layman's terms, this report means cancer cells are found; it is anaplastic grade III. Dr. Shapiro tells us he was able to get "all the tumor out in one lump chunk. But as for the cells, one just doesn't know, so you will have chemotherapy and radiation this time." Seems everyone is shocked, but I know it will be alright because God still knows what He's doing and I trust Him.

Even after surgery, while I'm recovering I continue to give the Lord praise for His marvelous workings through the skilled hands and minds of my physicians. I am in a semi-private room and my roommate finds it hard to believe that I've just had brain surgery. I tell her I have the best physicians and I'm blessed that God's not finished with me yet! I tell her of my book and she writes her address on the lunch napkin, asking me to let her know where to buy it. She wants to know the whole story.

> *But I trust in You, O Lord; I say, 'You are my God. My times are in Your hands...'*

(Psalm 31:14-15)

CHAPTER | 33

Another Divine Appointment, Not Coincidence

An interesting, "coincidence" happens after the second tumor is removed. I am attempting to order lunch at a wonderful deli shop downtown after one of my MRI appointments. Tom has to work on a computer issue at this restaurant which is across the street from the hospital. Call it divine fate or another coincidence -I say fate- but Dr. Sloan's mom is just ahead of me. She sees that I've had brain surgery and asks who did the operation. When I tell her, she tells me she's Dr. Sloan's mom. You will recall I had another *coincidental* meeting, one with Dr. Shapiro's mom three months after the first surgery in 2003. Now, here I stand next to Dr. Sloan's mom. In view of the other remarkable things happening in my life, no way is this merely a coincidence. *NO WAY.*

Ms. Sloan says, "That's my son over there." God's divine appointments are always in His perfect timing and I attest to this with first hand knowledge. It was actually her first time at that restaurant, too. How coincidental can things get before you have to know they are not coincidences?

I greet her doctor-son, introduce myself and hear him say, "You know, I thought you looked familiar!"

I tell him, "I bet I look a little bit different lying on that OR bed."

He takes a closer look at my skull and says, "It's healing up quite nicely!"

I reply, "I don't feel the burr holes as I did from the first surgery."

He replies, "I think I used a bone-filler with your surgery. I'd have to check my notes to make sure."

I thank him for using his God-given talents for my surgery. His mom tells me it's not often that she has the privilege of seeing the results of her son's work. She says, "It's great to see my son's hard work has paid off. You just look marvelous."

Dr. Sloan says, "Kim, it's great to see that you are doing so well." I thank him once more and hug him and his mom. All this can't be mere coincidence.

CHAPTER | 34

Radiation; A New Chapter

APRIL 21, 2005

Today I meet another physician along my journey, but this time it's for radiation and chemotherapy. Dr. Simon Lo is my radiation oncologist and his specialty is brain tumors. He's actually an assistant professor of his line of expertise. He tells me that radiation and chemotherapy when given together are the most significant way to fight my type of cancer. It was approved only two months ago – just in time for me. Not a coincidence; God's timing is always perfect. In the good and bad times I continue to give Him all the credit …and praise.

The Lord himself goes before you and will be with you; He will never leave you nor forsake you. Do not be afraid; do not be discouraged.

(Deuteronomy 31:8)

For I know the plans I have for you, declares the Lord, "plans to prosper you and not to harm you, plans to give you hope and a future.

(Jeremiah 29:11)

CHAPTER | 35

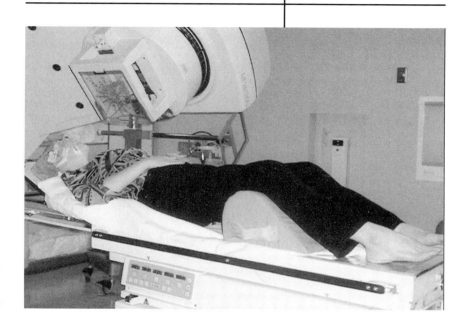

Radiation Mask

APRIL 28, 2005

At my first appointment I am fitted with a radiation mask. It begins as a flat, flexible piece of perforated plastic. It's made to fit by using laser lights when placed over my face to form a cast. Human hands make it fit exactly. I've always wondered what it would be like to have a twin sister and now I know. But really, is my chin that pointy?

This molded plastic replica is used as an instrument for my radiation therapist to administer the precise dose of treatment to the bed of my now-excised tumor on the chance that malignant cells may remain. If so, the radiation will destroy them.

CHAPTER | 36

Radiation Treatment

MAY 4, 2005

I don't know exactly what to expect in the first treatment. I ask my radiation technologist, Kent, many questions so I'll be well schooled about this procedure. I ask, "Will I feel anything during the treatment?"

He replies, "It won't hurt. But some people have told me they see a flash of blue light and experience some sort of a metallic smell." He tells me that my head and body must remain completely still as the radiation is being administered through a red beam of light. I ask how long each treatment lasts and how many I need to take.

He says, "About 15 minutes in total and you will come here to the hospital for seven weeks straight for five days a week. We give you the weekends off."

I reply, "Gee, Kent, thanks for the time off!" and we both chuckle.

Tom snaps a few pictures during this visit and first treatment. He takes the pictures just after the mask is made to fit and I make some

147

comment to him and Kent that I now know what it's like to have a twin... kind of. Kent tells me that I can take the mask home at the end of the seventh week. I thank him. I'm not sure where I'll put it but it will be a neat show-and-tell for this leg of my journey. I thought I had so many stories before! But now I have even more to share with others.

As our dear friend Mary shared with me to share with you in this book, "Kim was a child of God before brain surgery. But she has a passion to share with others her story of what God has done in her life."

I continue to trust and hope for the best possible outcome according to God's will. During this whole ordeal, I've been reading my Bible more and more. We have all trekked over rugged terrain but He continues to reveal how powerful He is when we place our trust in Him and in His will. I'm quite attentive without doubt; I know He is real. Through my experiences, He has been there even in the midst of the most difficult of times. With firsthand knowledge, I continue to proclaim that He provides comfort while we endure the most stressful of times. Even if we are uncertain of what our futures hold, He will never leave us. It is He who has all the answers. He has my time in His hands.

> *The Spirit of God has made me; the breath of the Almighty gives me life.*
> (Job 33:4)

> *Though You have made me see troubles...You will restore my life again; from the depth of the earth, You will again bring me up.*
> (Psalm 71:20)

> *Be joyful in hope, patient in affliction, faithful in prayer.*
> (Romans 12:12)

148

But I trust in You, O Lord; I say, 'You are my God.' My times are in Your hands...

(Psalm 31:14-15)

Now faith is being sure of what we hope for and certain of what we do not see.

(Hebrews 11:1)

Following the treatment, I tell Kent that I did smell something metallic and see that quick flash of a blue light when the radiation entered my head. "That *was* really weird." He tells me that some people experience it and some don't. He also informs me that with the radiation I will experience hair loss in the area being treated. My hair has just started to grow back but I most definitely can deal with the hair issue. It's just hair and if it gets to the point where it falls out then I'll have an excuse to wear wigs and choose my hair color and texture.

Today I break down and cry. Why am I crying? As I shower and wash my hair, I begin to cry out loud. I am careful to wash my hair in the treated area and even take Dr. Lo's advice by using baby shampoo. But, as I gently rub my scalp, I notice my new hair growth is now coming out in clumps. This is disturbing to me.

Side note here: It falls out exactly where my question mark scar is. But why cry? I know it will most likely grow back. There is only a slight chance it won't. But when it actually happens it's a whole new story.

Am I losing my hair for good? Will I always be wearing bandanas? I can see that I'm weakening. I'm thankful that God cares. This is just a season that I must endure. The time will almost certainly come when my hair will be healthy again. I suppose I will be sporting bandanas for a while. I'm told I look good in them, so it's

149

really not about my appearance; it's a reminder that I have cancer-ous cells in my brain. I will continue to lean on God for strength, especially with the next leg of my journey which is chemo.

For the next seven weeks I continue to have my radiation treatments as scheduled. During this time, I have the privilege to meet so many faces. I've met many "new friends" during my wait in the waiting area. I've seen some really bad cases of depression. I have had many opportunities to share my story and most are amazed that I'm doing so well. But I tell them of my faith that it is the work of the Lord. I've even prayed with a few patients and family members right there in the waiting area before their treatments. It's something that is new to me, but I see this as a "God thing." And I know I've been blessed with the ability to communicate, and so I open my mouth and tell about my journey.

I also tell about my book. I've collected many names and phone numbers of family members of people I just happen to cross paths with in everyday life. Many say they'd like to have copies. I keep these names in order to help them get the books. It is not my nature to preach; I just tell my journey and how the Lord has been with me all the way. I'm really an ordinary person who has experienced an extraordinary measure of peace and strength from our Creator in my travail, and I just want to share it with others.

One elderly patient whom I met today has esophagus cancer. She is told she needs surgery for her cancer but she refuses to "let them cut on her."

"Ain't nobody gonna open me up," she boldly proclaims. "That's why you got that cancer again because you let them open your head up that first time and it spread now." This has caught me off guard; it's a bizarre allegation.

Then there are those who have said, "I'm amazed that you're doing so well, having gone through two brain surgeries, let alone getting through them with small children to take care of. Stay strong, Girl, keep your great spirit. Keep your faith strong. You've been through so much for someone so young. Most people never experience half of what you have in their lifetimes." I'm always quick to tell them it's all God and it's His strength.

I've found that there are some really scared folks here because of their physical aliments. I would say a majority seem not to have faith in the higher power. They appear to feel helpless as I did at first during my storm. They seem to treat their sickness as if there is no hope at all, a death sentence. I know about fear. But I trust God; He is my strength. I wish for all who are hurting or who are fearful to know this same assurance.

The Lord is my light and my salvation whom shall I fear?
The Lord is the stronghold of my life of whom shall I be
afraid?

(Psalm 27:1)

I have become friends with my new nurses, doctors and radiation techs at Indiana University Medical Center in the basement of the Cancer Pavilion. There are a lot of great folks here to help all of us who depend on their expertise. I'm very blessed to have met such great people. I have become acquainted with more people today. Kim, Stephanie and Angela will set up my treatments this time. I tell Kim I like her name. She smiles and says some of her friends even call her Kimmie. I tell her it's the same with me. She is quite nice and has beautiful blue eyes. She asks what type of music I like and I tell her. So she says, "I have this new CD; I think you would like it."

151

She plays it. I do like it and ask, "Who is this singing?"

She says, "It's Jack Johnson. Would you believe he's a surfer from Hawaii?"

I tell her, "Yes, I can believe it. Wow, but I didn't know those guys could sing so well! I'll have to get this CD!"

Side note: Whenever she was my tech, she knew exactly which CD to play for me. It was played on a counter top rather than through any headphones.

After many consecutive days of treatment, I meet many of my new techs. I begin baking cookies to show my appreciation for their help. But then again I don't want to get them too spoiled. They all deserve the added sweetness because of all of the love and compassion they show me. I'm known to them now as, "Kim the Cookie Lady" and one new nurse I've never met says to me as I pass her in the hallway, "Your smile is contagious. It can be stressful here but when I see your smiling face, I smile!" I find that as a great compliment to my Creator since He is the One that keeps me smiling even when things are tough!

I've said it before and I'll say it again, "It's all about Him, not about Kim!"

Side note: When I arrive for my appointments I've been observant, noticing they look at my hands to see if I've brought any cookies. It's a joy for me to still be able to do what I love and to show them love. I bake the night before my early morning treatments.

Other patients in the cancer waiting room tell me about the different experiences through their respective journeys through chemotherapy, mostly negative stories. They look so tired and worn. Some tell of their feelings about losing all their hair, some saying it

152

never grew back. Some say they always had straight hair and had always wished it were wavy and after chemo they got their wishes: wavy hair. Many tell of how they had lost their sense of taste as well as their appetites. One man advises me not to eat anything I really like because after chemo is over I may grow to dislike that food entirely. Many tell of how they got extremely thin. Boy, this really is going to be tough, but I know the Lord is much tougher.

I continue to trust because there isn't a thing anyone can do without the will of the Lord. I'm helpless but not hopeless. I'm extremely thankful that I've had this time to visit with other cancer survivors because I've learned a lot about how people handle their difficult times. It is a life experience I'd never trade.

CHAPTER | 37

CHEMO Experience

MAY 6, 2005

Next, as planned, is chemotherapy in pill form, not through an IV. I'm at home, it's 10:00 p.m. May 5th, 2005, and I am led to pray just prior to taking the five pills. Down the hatch they go and I am falling asleep. Now it's 3:00 a.m. May 6th and I wake up to this gurgling feeling in my stomach and this overwhelming feeling that I am going to throw-up. I run to the bathroom and "There she blows!" I am the sickest I've ever been in my entire life! I am not only sicker than a dog, I probably don't know what it's like to be a dog, but I do know I am crawling around on the floor like one. I am so weak and nauseous that I think, "this is it, my last day here on earth!"

Tom hears me crying out for God's mercy. Of course, it's the chemo pills. I was told that there might be some side effects and given a prescription for anti-nausea medicine, it was left up to me whether to take it. I chose not to, hoping to be one of those who don't experience the sickness. That was a big mistake!

Now I experience the worst side effects and it appears my body is unable to cope. I just can't stop vomiting and having the runs. I'm feeling that I need to have some fluids in my system but I know it will only make things worse.

Tom is feeling helpless in this moment of desperation. He does the only the thing he knows how to do best and that is to pray for me. He prays and sings songs of praise and worship and they bring comfort. Tom truly is my Godsend. Fifteen years of splendid marriage. God, the perfect matchmaker "(made) me a match…" that would have the love, compassion, patience and wonderful heart with which Tom was created. God knew of this journey I would trek and that I would need Tom.

After a while I am able to get to our whirlpool bathtub and I soak, just trying to relax, plus I read somewhere that when your body is dehydrated the best way to hydrate fast is to lie in a tub so the pores can soak up the water. This treatment from the whirlpool/hot tub reminds me of when I attempted to get rid of my headache during the vacation in Chicago. It's ironic how my life seems to be coming around full circle.

I continue to feel less than human. It is now time to get the kids off to school, but I stay in the tub. How will I endure this suffering? Our kids come in to kiss me goodbye. I find myself examining each one of them and I mentally take pictures of how I'll remember them. Is this the very last time I will see my kids? I'm starting to feel extreme weariness. They all witness my crying from the pain and say, "Mommy, we hope you feel better."

I kiss them all one by one as they are about to leave. As I kiss them I have this ominous thought, "Maybe this *will* be my last time I will see them." But quickly my negative thinking becomes positive and I think, "Today is the first day of the rest of my life! God isn't finished with me yet. I shall live!"

Tom gets the kids to school and also takes Spencer to Tom's sister's home so she can take him to his afternoon kindergarten class at

Kingsway Christian School while we are at the hospital. Fortunately, she is just one block away from our house. While Tom is gone I continue to pray and try to muster the strength just to dress myself. I am just too weak even to want to get out of the tub. I literally ask God for an extra measure of strength so I can get ready to go to the E.R. wearing clothes and not just this robe.

I can truly attest that feeling this weak and ill, I really don't care about looks; just get me to the hospital, clothes or no clothes.

Tom is home now and is literally lifting me out of the tub and helping me dress. Tom will literally carry me to our van.

I ask him to grab a bucket just in case I need it on the way to the hospital. The drive seems longer than the normal 25 minutes. The bad part is I have the "dry heaves" which only make this trip much worse. I am mentally and physically exhausted.

Tom gets me to my oncologist's office. My nurse, Candy, is wonderfully compassionate and I need her. She helps me to the restroom and there I vomit again. She rubs my back and gets me into a wheelchair. Dr. Lo, Candy, Tom and I head to the ER. I'm pale as a ghost. Comfort is the gift that is given to me during this hospitalization at the Indiana University Medical Center.

Dr. Lo asks the ER nurse to inject some anti-nausea meds into my veins. I'm told I'm totally dehydrated, which I know to be true. My legs and knees are shaking so violently and I haven't the faintest idea how or when I shall ever get back to my normal self. Am I cold? Am I going to get better? Am I going to live past this moment? After literally crying out for strength, I have an overwhelming sense that, yes, I'm going to live. I shall live to see our children grow to be adults. I'll attend their weddings. God's purpose for me is not complete. How do I know this? Because of this peace from God that has suddenly enveloped me. I know this is not my strength at all. It's from a higher place.

"Peace I leave with you; My peace I give you…" (John 14:27).

Now, I'm in my ER bed and the attendants make me somewhat comfortable. My new nurse starts me on an IV drip for hydration. I'm also receiving an anti-nausea IV. It's been a while and the drug still seems not to have taken affect; though I am somewhat improved, I am still very sick. One more IV drug is administered. Now, after an hour, I feel that this one is easing the nausea. My nurse and Tom are happy to see that I'm starting to feel better. I actually take a nap.

I've been here for about six hours and the medical people release me with a prescription to treat the nausea problem so I can continue my chemotherapy. I tell my doctor, "I don't know if I can." It's now a mental thing. I've seen my darkest days with the side effects and it's going to be hard to convince my mind to continue with this regimen. He assures me that I must continue. I'm told that if I can make it through the first three days, then I'll be fine for the rest of the time. I reluctantly agree to continue; I must because of the possibility of remaining cancer cells. My doctors are with me for this journey and I know they are only looking out for my best interests. Besides, I'm in the best of care in another way that "exceeds all understanding."

We pick up the prescription and head home. Tom really takes loving care of me. It's almost 9:00 p.m., time for me to take the pills again. I take the anti-nausea pill one hour prior to taking the chemo pills. I am nervous about a reoccurrence of the devastation, but I'm finally brave enough and down the hatch that anti-nausea pill goes. At 10:00 p.m., I ask Tom if he and I can pray together and we do. I take the five chemo pills and hope and pray for the best!

CHAPTER | 38

It's a New Day!

It's May 7, 2005, and I've just awakened; what time is it? 9:00 a.m. I've slept the whole night through. I feel great! It really is amazing how such a tiny pill can make such a huge difference. I don't feel a bit nauseous. I sense that I can make it through the 12 months on this drug regimen just fine. I can do this only because I know that when I'm weak, He makes me stronger! It's another promise He gives…and *keeps*. He is powerful!

> … *'My grace is sufficient for you, for My power is made perfect in weakness'…For when I am weak, than I am strong.*
>
> *(*2 Corinthians 12:9-10)

God plans my journey through life, and cancer is part of that journey. I feel my time in the hospital with other cancer patients is exactly how it is meant to be. I would have never had the many opportunities to meet so many hurting and wonderful people. We all had something in common, cancer of some sort in our bodies. Without this tumor, I doubt that I could have so fully known God's love, mercy and proper plan for my journey through life – which clearly now is far from finished.

There are many family members who hardly have any strength left to care for their loved ones. Maybe it's literally God's purpose for me to show them that He provides the comfort they need while they are in these low valleys; that He will lead them to the mountain tops if they believe. I believe God is using me to bring comfort in the most uncomfortable of times to these patients who need encouragement. I've experienced so much negativity while sitting in the waiting area. I've listened to all the sad stories and the helplessness in their voices.

I've been there and done that: two major brain surgeries, the second involving cancer. I can talk with practically anyone another characteristic I share with my Paw. I tend to think on the positive side. To me, "the glass is half full, not half empty." Perhaps I am one of God's messengers meant to spread hope among those who have not yet completed their journeys through this valley of fear. And, of course, I do have the "gift of gab."

CHAPTER | 39

Last Radiation Treatment

JUNE 22, 2005

After seven weeks and a total of 35 radiation treatments, I've begun the final one. I'm somewhat sad, in a way, that I'm on my final treatment. Why? I'm kind of sad, because I will never see my waiting room friends again, but I hope I have helped bring some encouragement into the storms they are facing. I shall make every effort to come see the nurses and my oncologist, Dr. Simon Lo, when I'm here for my MRI appointments.

Here at the hospital there is a ritual for cancer patients on completion of their treatments. It entails ringing a gold bell in the front lobby. It's now my turn and I ring it with three bold tugs. The staff that I've grown to love and appreciate all applaud and some are crying tears of joy. Some new patients smile at me and say, "Great job!"

I think to myself, "Hmmm…I didn't do a thing, it's just a journey." I believe God made the doctors with their knowledge for all of us who are in need and I also believe in medicine, a derivative of His divinity. With radiation, the only side effects I've had are that I'm tired and lack the energy I had before. My hair is slowly thinning. I have to be sure to stay out of the direct sunlight without having protection on my head – thus I have every color of bandana Wal-Mart sells. Sometimes I'm grumpy, forgetful of important dates and times.

Currently, I'm blessed with the strength still to be able to do my normal routines but just not as swiftly as before radiation. I'm thankful that I still have the ability to wash clothes and do dishes. Yes, don't take those tasks for granted! I just saw on a billboard at a church that hit it right on: "Enjoy this day, compliments of your Creator." I am enjoying each moment. I'm learning not to take life for granted because really we don't know when it's our time to leave this world.

CHAPTER | 40

Seasons Change

AUGUST 2006

Looking back on all that has transpired I have a much clearer view of life and a much richer appreciation of all He has created: family, friends, rain, snow, and even the leaves that fall in autumn. Even little things in life happen for reasons, much like the seasons we experience. Living in Indiana all my 40 years now, I have experienced stormy times in the early spring; tornadoes and heavy rains hit hard. Just as with the weather-related storms, we have physical storms over which we have little or no control, but He does.

We shall always have storms to walk through. These times are our times to reflect and see how strong our faith is. Just knowing that the storm will pass helps to view it in a positive light. The sun does come back and shine. The rain is needed for growth, much like the physical storms we must endure help us grow, especially spiritually. Think about it: "Into each life some rain must fall" for a very good reason. The Creator knew best!

By now you know I've learned that I need to trust in His promises, rest in His care, and serve in the shadow of His strength. I've learned to focus on Him and not the problems!

Though You have made me see troubles, many and bitter, You will restore my life again; from the depth of the earth You will again bring me up.

(Psalm 71:20)

You will keep in perfect peace him whose mind is steadfast, because he trusts in You. Trust in the Lord forever, for the Lord, is the Rock eternal.

(Isaiah 26:3-4)

May the Lord of peace Himself give you peace at all times and in every way.

(2 Thessalonians 3:16)

Whoever believes in Me, as the Scripture has said, streams of living water will flow from within him.

(John 7:38)

Seasons come and go but the love of God is forever!

CHAPTER | 41

New News...

OCTOBER 2006

My mom noticed that dad hasn't been eating normally and decides that he needs to go in for a check up. The doctor found that he has a "leaky heart valve" and may have had it from birth. Coincidently, you might say, Teese is in town for a Bridal Fair that Amy asked her to attend. Bridal Fair? Well, remember Amy, my youngest sister whom I was trying to set up with Dr. Miller before my first brain surgery? Well, she has met the love of her life. Johnathon and she have been talking about getting married next May, 2007.

At Dad's check up they take a couple vials of blood to test. It all turns out to be relatively normal. But, he continues to feel weak, so Teese says, "He needs a CT scan!" His doctor orders one. The results will be back in a few days.

I drive Mom to his doctor's a couple days later and we request his results. We are told to wait and they will retrieve them. After waiting almost an hour, I boldly go to his doctor's nurse and tell her we aren't leaving until we get the results. Sounds very similar to the scenario when I went for my first CT orders at a different hospital. One thing I've noticed since my brain surgeries is that I'm more bold and determined than ever before.

His nurse hands me the typed report; I begin to read it. I'm well schooled about these reports because of my own CT experiences. While reading, I can hardly hold back the tears. I look at Mom and say, "Mom, Teese, it's not good news." This reminds me of when my own Dr. Meng told me of my first brain tumor. Now, I too must deliver the news that Paw has cancer. Dear Lord, what a shock! I read the report to them and tell them that not only does he have cancer, but it's spread to all lobes of his liver, both lungs, the right kidney, spleen, and colon.

How can this be? We three are just floored with the news. We are crying but now I must be strong and call my brother so he can drive the ten minutes from home to bring Paw to this office. Despite the news I am able to gather my composure and remain calm over the phone even though there is a storm inside me. I stoically tell Steve that the doctor needs to see Paw. He says he'll be here in ten minutes. I call Amy and say the same and she, too, is on her way.

I know how important family is during a time as serious as this. We need to be together. The strength will only come from God, the strength to cope with this dreadful development. We are a loving, close family. This would be extremely difficult on our own but we aren't on our own. God is with us when we go through these fiery trials.

I wait patiently for them as I stand at the front door of this office building. I'm on the inside looking out. I keep my emotions low-key, but I don't want to be the one to bring the news.

Paw, Steve and Amy have arrived and I join them as we walk into the consultation room; Mom and Teese are already there. Steve notices our having cried and I'm sure he is wondering what's going on. Such rooms are all too familiar to me. Even though it's a totally different place they serve the same purpose when we receive news about our health.

His doctor now knocks on the door, comes in and delivers the news. "Clayton, you have cancer and it doesn't look good." Tears don't come to Paw's eyes-yet. Does he not hear what his doctor is saying? Yes, he hears. I know exactly where Paw's mind is right now, having walked this cancer path myself. At the moment, Dad is in La La Land. We all are crying, but Paw, Steve and Amy don't even know how bad it is yet.

His doctor continues to deliver the news without showing any emotion. I ask, "Paw, do you understand the seriousness of what he is saying?"

He immediately replies, "Yes. But he doesn't act as though he cares by saying it so matter-of-factly. "Let me put it to ya'll this way: it's like someone just knocked me off my feet and knocked the wind out of me." Now dad's tears are running like water as ours are. He then confidently says, "God is with me and can heal me. He can do anything He wants. He has the power!" He holds on to all he has learned about faith and hope, and his is in the Lord. I've been there twice with the brain tumors and Paw's been right there by my side as my daddy. It serves as a great example of his faith.

He and Mom brought us kids up to know the Lord and His book of faith. His doctor tries to console him and says, "I do care and believe me; I'm sorry to have to give you this news."

Steve blurts out loud, I suppose, in his own La La Land mind and in his disbelief and frustration, "I don't understand! We were just in Disney back in June and he walked the entire park and rode all the rides. And then you tested his blood last week and it all turned out within normal range. Now, how could the cancer not show up in those tests?"

The doctor is almost at a loss for words, but says he can have more tests run to check for sure. He is as stunned as we. He sees that my dad has no outward signs that anything is wrong with him. I'm sure it must be difficult for doctors to bring bad news to patients.

Dad has more tests including a colonoscopy a few days later and cancer is found. Colon cancer is the primary source. Much in the manner that mine was ruled as a primary brain tumor, we are told that his type of cancer can and has spread. I ask how long has it been there, and his new doctor says, "Well, it takes eight to ten years to develop in the colon and his is already oozing blood from what I see in the scope. Because this is a hereditary disease, all of his children will need to have a colonoscopy performed."

We can't wait until age fifty, the normal rule of thumb to have one done. He says colon cancer is the most treatable kind if it's caught early. We can't believe it!

That's a long time to have something wrong and not even have any signs of it. The only outward sign to us has been that his eating has slowly been decreasing. Otherwise, we would not have known anything health-wise was wrong with him. Much like my high pain-tolerance with the tumors and just having the headache. I most certainly know where I get the high pain-tolerance gene, my Paw. He always has said I'm just like him. In many ways I am.

168

God has a way of getting our attention. He designed us all differently and that's what makes us His own creation.

After getting the news that his cancer is incurable since it's in his liver and other organs, we are all spending more quality time with him. He's talking up a storm lately a journey down memory lane. He has begun talking about the pet monkey he had while growing-up in North Carolina. As he sits on the tan leather couch downstairs at home, he surprises Steve and me with what he says next: "I love all my children and I'm so proud of you all. I even love the baby I never got to hold in my arms or rock in a chair."

Side note: The baby he's referring to is our brother, Jeffrey, who was stillborn and full term. His airways were cut off as he traveled down the birth canal and he died.

Dad has always loved rocking babies and I remember his rocking Amy and me to sleep as well as my own children. He loved to rock his kids in rocking chairs while cuddling us to sleep. Is he trying to give us information to hold-on to that he's held deep inside? Seems like it.

Today at his appointment, I talk with Paw's cancer specialist and tell her of Amy's wedding plans. She turns to Amy and says, "Amy, I understand that you are planning a wedding. That's wonderful, congratulations." She then tells us, "Amy, if you want your dad to be at your wedding, you better get married this Saturday. I wouldn't wait. He's very sick and may not have much longer."

Because of Teese's already being here for this Bridal Fair, Amy has selected her wedding dress. She also has Johnathon's and her wedding rings. Johnathon asked Dad and Mom for their blessing for marrying her some time ago. They both agreed and are extremely pleased with this union because they trust that the Lord has brought these two young people together and the two of them have long awaited this union. Paw even tells me what he has told Johnathon: "Welcome to the family!" That is so Paw. So, loving, accepting and caring; only wants the best for his children, and Amy has been blessed with a good Christian man. He is the knight in shining armor for whom she has longed.

Weeks go by and Paw isn't his normal self. Seems he's dealing with the thought of his illness and with the reality of what's to come. He is crying out to God in the middle of the night, "Lord, I love my wife. God please heal me!" He keeps crying out, "Momma." Amy, Teese and I all witness this. We go to him and pray. I can feel God's presence in his room.

Teese says to us, "Mom said that she has been praying that he will see his mom and dad in heaven." And now, here is our father calling out as if his momma and daddy were not far off in the distance. He was born and reared in the South - precisely in North Carolina. And, from my earliest recollection, he addressed her as "Momma."

This startles me because I tell about my dream just last night. I dreamed I saw Grandma Manning; she was smiling with her famous gap in the middle teeth (a trait that Amy inherited) and with her beautiful white hair that people complimented her on when we went out with her. I saw her with out-stretched arms. She was calling out, "Clayton." This brings me to my knees as I tell my family because I use to dream of Grandma but it has been a long time since I have had any dreams of her.

We go to him and pray over him. We are holding him as if he were our baby embracing him with the love that's as pure just as a love for a newborn baby. He's our Paw and we love him so much. He's the best dad and of course we hate to see him like this. He says, "If you knew how much I hurt..." and he continues to weep. I don't think he is in physical pain; the pain he's referring to is the fear of being separated from us. He says, "I don't want to leave your mom." It's as if he knows something.

Dad has always had this way of knowing things through his dreams, especially during the last five years. As a perfect example, a few years ago I received a long-awaited call. It was from my son Matt's adoptive dad. He called to tell me that Matt wants to meet us; it surely is sooner than I had thought it would be. The interesting coincidence is Dad had already told me this news two days prior to my even getting that call. I remember Dad saying years ago that he had a dream that he saw his grandson Matt, the son I gave for adoption. He felt assured that we would get to meet him and it would be much sooner than we all think. I recall hoping that it really would be just as in Dad's dream. Dad knew and I believe it was the Lord's showing Him through his dreams.

> *...your old men will dream dreams, your young men will see visions.*
>
> (Joel 2:28)

Side note: We have all had the grand reunion of meeting Matt numerous times during the past three and a half years. It's been such a wonderful blessing to spend time with him.

Back to Dad going down memory lane, he says, "Did I ever tell you about playing baseball when I was a boy? I played with a couple boys named Catfish Hunter and Gaylord Perry. They went on to make it in the major league. Gaylord married a Manning girl. No kin to us that I know of at least."

I say, "Yeah, Dad, I remember your telling me of those days."

Still being visibly upset, we now sing to him; he has always wanted to hear us sing together. Well, tonight we are giving him a gospel concert. He continues to enjoy it. We distinctly hear a compliment: "It is beautiful to hear all my girls singing. I've always wanted to hear you three sing together." We are touched that Dad is feeling joy. Like a newborn baby, He falls asleep. It's a most peaceful sleep. Hey, something else; he doesn't snore anymore. This is amazing since he has snored for as long as I can remember and that's a long, long time.

Later on he tells us he doesn't like the idea of changing the wedding day because it makes him feel that we don't think he'll be around until the original marriage date. We just tell him we want him to be able to enjoy it with the family all together. He's okay with the decision now.

We drive him to Macy's Department Store to select and purchase a new suit and tie since he's lost so much weight and nothing fits him now. He has such a kind and knowledgeable older man fit him correctly for his new suit. He always wore a suit to church, but they just didn't fit anymore. Not even the smaller ones he had in his closet.

Paw surely looks stunning in his new suit. I can hardly wait to see him for the wedding, which by the way, is less than a week away. Being a bargain hunter as is he, I think how we can save some money on this purchase. I remember there is a coupon in the newspaper at home but that's just it; it's at home. Wonder if they have any extras? That's one of the many things Paw has taught me, "You won't know until you ask. Don't be bashful." So, with my boldness, I ask the cashier if he has an extra coupon.

172

He replies, "No, I'm sorry I don't."

But then, out of the blue, a female shopper hears me and says to the salesman, "Excuse me, but I have one. Can they use mine?"

He says, "Absolutely." I smile and thank her. Wow, just by asking for this coupon has saved a whole $40. I tell my family who are next to me, "Hey, that's $40 and $40 is $40.

Amy smiles and says, "Yes, you are right. I just don't know how you do it. Good going there, Kim."

As Paw sits in the wheelchair, he says, "Good job, Kim!" I smile and say, "Thank you Paw. I learned it from the best." He smiles and I kiss his cheek.

As we make our way to the elevator, a lady stops us. She surely looks familiar. I hear, "Clayton! Do you remember me from teaching your Adult Sunday School at Abundant Life Church?"

He looks up and says, "Why, shucks, of course I do. You're Mae Moody."

Teese, Mom, Steve, Amy and I look and all remember and hug her. We say, "Mae, you haven't aged a day, just like the ageless Dick Clark." She says, "I don't know about that" and chuckles.

She is here literally in God's perfect timing. We tell her about his disease and she is sorry to hear of it. She shares her family's health issues with us and is quick to remind us all of God's promises. She gives us peaceful and positive thoughts to remember.

She reminds us of God's promises and that Heaven is our real home not earth.

Teese asks, "Mae, would you pray for our dad?" And she does, right here in the shopping area near the elevator. She is a wonderful lady and is a preaching minister on the south-side of Indianapolis. She finishes and adds, "Clayton, you never missed a day of Sunday School. You were so faithful."

He smiles and says, "I know even back in the blizzard of 76, my little '72 Volkswagen Beetle bug got us there each Sunday." She smiles and says, "Oh, yes, I remember your orange bug." He was the exact same way at Western Electric, where he retired. He never missed a day of work. He worked there 36 years and in that length of time I know he surely touched many lives and I know many of his friends. He was nick-named "Rebel" because he was the first southern gentleman at Western Electric.

CHAPTER | 42

A Wedding in a Week

The time has arrived and Amy and Johnathon are getting married at the Abundant Life Church. This is her church and also where we grew up to know the Lord. Since Teese is here, the wedding is a great success and all the decorating looks fantastic! This is a combination of many talents from family, church family, friends and co-workers of both of them. It will and has taken a "God Thing" to pull this wedding together. Pastor Bosworth will perform the ceremony and his wife is serving as wedding coordinator. It looks as though the wedding has been planned for months. It all flows so beautifully. It's truly a "God thing."

"With man this is impossible but with God all things are possible."

Paw is present in his wheelchair. The extended family is present including my brother-in-law Mark, niece Anne, and nephew Mark.

Also present are Bob, Chris, Matt and Cheri. They are Matt's adoptive family who drove eight hours to be here for Paw and Amy. They stay with us and continue to cherish the time they have with Paw. This is one more opportunity for Matt and his family to spend more quality, valuable time together. It's really hard to believe time goes by so quickly.

One memorable time we had together was just five months earlier in May 2006 when Bob, Matt's dad treated Dad and me to a Pacer's game with the two of them when they were in Indy visiting with us. This is most memorable to Matt as well; he has said he thinks it was really cool. He is able to continue visiting Grandpa Manning and is grateful he has this relationship with him. Matt tells me, "He taught me a lot in the short time since I've got to know him. I look forward to being with him even more." This time is extra special to Paw, as he has personally told me. He's glad to have pictures of that day at the Pacer's game with which to reminisce. We have great, fond and fun memories of our times together.

Not only are Matt's favorite teams in the leagues of the Indiana Pacers and the Indianapolis Colts but they are Paw's too. Once I was present with Dad when we went into the Fishers, Indiana post office. So many folks know him when they see him. On one occasion I saw workers greet him and one said, "Clayton, how's your nephew Peyton doing?"

Paw replied, "He's doing mighty fine!" and they exchanged smiles.

I turned to dad and whispered, "We aren't related to Peyton Manning of the Colts, are we?"

He says, "I'm not for sure but he is from the south and I'll claim him." Dad is such a jovial man.

Now, getting back to the wedding... We are all seated. Paw and Amy hold hands as our loving brother, Steve, wheels the black and silver chair that Paw sits in down the center aisle. I can't help but think back that not only is this same center aisle I walked down to accept Christ, but also it's the same one I walked

176

with him some 16 years ago during my wedding with Tom. The only difference is Paw is in the wheel chair and isn't walking as he was during our wedding. He's smiling. It's still a very proud moment for him. I look around and there's not a dry eye in the church of 100 or more of friends and relatives who are here to celebrate this union. God is faithful and we are grateful.

Paw is so pleased with the union of Amy and Johnathon; He has told me many times how happy he is for them. He says to Johnathon, "You know I love you. And I know you will take care of Amy." This marriage brings such joy to our daddy's heart and tears of joy to his and Mom's eyes. I know because I'm directly behind them in this pew. I am taking pictures with my digital camera. So is my sister in law Anna Lou whose pictures are professional. She has always been a great photographer. We are blessed by agreeing to photograph Amy & Johnathon's wedding on such short notice. Once again, God is generous and we are grateful.

I can hardly believe that game was almost a year ago this May.
Seasons do change but for our growth. Amen!

178

CHAPTER | 43

Hospice Stay

It's now been almost a month since the diagnosis and a little over a week since the wedding. Mom decides it might be time to call the hospice and ask for help. The hospice nurse is now on her way over here to the house.

Paw's not doing well today. As a matter of fact, he's barely been responsive all day. I call the hospice and ask, "How much longer will it be before the nurse gets here?" The nurse has been delayed by a major traffic jam.

The doorbell rings and she is here. As she observes Paw she says, "Oh, boy!" I know that can't be a good thing from the tone of her voice.

She takes Mom and the rest of us upstairs and says, "Peggy, I think you should consider letting us take him to Hospice." It's really hard for Mom and all of us children to come to the reality that Paw is actually nearing his life's finale. He has been so full of life. The nurse asks Mom what we would like to do. Fighting back her emotions, Mom replies, "I'll put it this way, I don't want to come downstairs and find him dead. "Yes, I think you are right. It's time for Hospice. Maybe they can run more tests on him." As I hear Mom's words, I truly realize that she's holding on

179

to him for dear life. She is in total denial about how sick he is. It's La La Land once again, the place we go when we don't want to deal with reality. The nurse takes mom's hand and says in a tender loving way, "Peggy, he is actively dying. He's not going to get better." It's reality and extremely sad."

The nurse orders a Hospice room for him, stat. She informs us that she will also call for an ambulance to take him so we won't have to deal with getting him in and out of the car. The ambulance arrives almost 40 minutes late because of the rush hour traffic.

Mom rides with Paw, but in the front seat and we kids follow behind in our car to watch for any signs of movement as we can see him through the back windows in the ambulance doors. We arrive and they get him into his bed. He's on liquid morphine so I assume that he will be out of it for a while.

He's in and out of knowing what's happening. We tell him he is in a hospital. We choose not to use the word, "Hospice" since his older brother Johnnie passed away recently. Uncle Johnnie had spent his last days in between the hospice and the hospital with Paw visiting him before he passed away. Paw says he thinks he feels as though he's getting better. This is familiar to me from my own days in the hospital with the surgeries on my brain. Positive thinking is what Paw and I have in common with regard to our days in the hospital.

At a recent Sunday church service I am quick to think about what our pastor Jim Burks spoke on. Our days are numbered so we should make them count. I'm certain that Paw has made them count. He taught us many life lessons as we were growing up and even now as adults we are still learning many life lessons from him. To God be all the glory!

180

We are staying with him round the clock and it's getting harder to deal with the reality that Dad isn't getting any better. Pastor Bosworth comes to visit and so does our minister, Pastor Burks, as well as more friends and family. Paw is un-responsive.

At one point my curiosity makes me ask his nurse, "Is he in a coma?"

She says, "No." Then she says something along the lines of: "This is one of the effects of morphine. We try to keep our patients comfortable." He does seem peaceful.

Last night I had a dream. I dreamed that all of us kids and mom will sing happy birthday to him. We are all in his room, including a family friend, Dave, and whom our Paw nick-named years ago, "Dr. Dave." Also present are Amanda, Amy's best friend since high school, our Indiana Manning cousins (Debbie & Johnnie) and our Aunt Nina, Dad's brother's widow. Since we are all present I blurt out what happened in my dream from last night. Afterwards, I say, "Everybody: one, two, three - hit it! Happy birthday to you…" We smile and sing and I sense dad is hearing. The nurse has said hearing is usually the last thing to go so she thinks he hears us.

This is a grand day! I prayed dad would make it to see his birthday and he has! He's still unresponsive, though. It's sad because for all our birthdays, mom has always celebrated with a wonderful lunch, then cake, candles and ice cream, singing that same song; the whole nine yards. But this one is being celebrated in a hospice room. We are celebrating his life and he is still with us and we are certainly blessed to be able to see this day.

Tom brings the kids to the hospice today for the first time since Paw has been here. We're not quite sure how to address their curiosity but it ends up being quite a pleasant visit.

Rachel, our nine-year-old daughter - Paw's granddaughter drew a picture on a card she made for his birthday and gives it to him while they visit and she tells him what it's a picture of. She says, "Paw, I drew you a picture for your birthday and it's a picture of Calvin, Collin, Spencer and me. It's of you, sitting in your new wheel chair." I say, "It's a beautiful drawing Sis. It sure looks like Paw is carrying that wheelchair and he looks strong."

"Be strong and courageous for the Lord your God will be with you wherever you go."

She is very loving and shows her love through acts of kindness. She has such a beautiful heart and truly is a creative and self-taught artist. She kisses his cheek and says, "Happy Birthday Grandpa. We love you." Then Tom, Calvin, Collin and Spencer echo the same and kiss his cheek. I wish he would hug them back but he's too sedated by the medication.

Spencer, our youngest, and being only six years old, turns to Grandma and in his sweet, innocent, young voice says, "Grandma, is Paw just sleepy?"

She says, "Yes, he's very sleepy right now. He's had a rough night." Mom kisses each of them and walks Rachel's picture over to the cork board on the wall and fastens it into the cork with the push pin.

Chapter | 44

A New Season

The next day this same thought hits me the more we visit Paw: I see dad and he is physically here with us all but it's just his body lying in a hospice bed. That's not the normal, happy-go-lucky, full-of-energy-and fun dad and grandpa he has always been. It's his body lying there. It surely doesn't look as though it's going to be much longer to me since his body just looks so lifeless. He looks as though he is ready for his heavenly home to take over from his earthly home. This saddens me deeply but I know that God didn't design bodies to last on earth forever. I'm thankful we sang to him yesterday and told him how much we love him because now he seems to be taking a turn for the worse. For the past few days he has remained unresponsive and Mom refuses to leave his side. She loves him and they recently celebrated their 54th wedding anniversary.

> *Why you do not even know what will happen tomorrow. What is your life? You are a mist that appears for a little while and then vanishes.*
>
> (James 4:14)

I'm treasuring this time with him. I continue to talk to him and go down memory lane despite his non-communicative state. I know he hears me. I even tested the theory by asking him to squeeze my fingers if he could hear me after I spoke to him. He did squeeze them. I'm grateful that he knows we are right by his side and that he's loved immeasurably.

It's now getting late and somehow between the nurse and us kids we are able to convince Mom to go home to get rest this evening because she needs it badly. It's after 10 p.m. as I drive Mom home. It's a short distance, about 15 to 20 minutes. We arrive and talk a little while and I say, "I'll be home with you tonight and we'll head back to the Hospice first thing in the morning; How does that sound, Mom?"

"That sounds like a good plan," she replies. She and I put our pajamas on; We know we need some serious sleep. We have got very little sleep during the past few days. Mom is a great mother and a wonderful wife to Paw. God knew best in joining them together.

I've observed her keeping his lips and mouth hydrated by using this green sponge. She dips it into the cold water day in and day out. It resembles a toothbrush on a stick. Her love language is very apparent in her actions. By nature she is a quiet lady. As the old saying goes, "Actions speak louder than words"; it's true. She cares for Paw so patiently, lovingly and compassionately just as she has for us kids. I know she would have been a wonderful nurse had she chosen that career.

Right after we get home the phone rings. My heart leaps; I think the worse has happened. It's Amy who says, "I don't think Paw is doing well." The nurse says it doesn't appear that he has much longer to live because his skin is starting to marble. That's usually a sign that his circulation isn't good. It's normally an indication that the body is getting ready to shut down.

184

I say that we will be there and I hang up. I'm crying as I say to Mom, "We need to get back up to the Hospice. Amy says the nurse thinks he doesn't have much longer and she knows we want to be with him: We get our clothes on and head out the door as fast as humanly possible. We are really in La La Land as we head to the Hospice.

Mom tells me, "Be careful driving. Don't speed." I give her a line she used back when I was a teenager and trying to tell her how to drive one day. Back then I thought I knew it all; especially since I had just finished taking Drivers Education.

I say, "I have my drivers license, and guess what? It even has my picture on it." That was such a classic line, I remember as though it was yesterday. But reality is she used it on me many years ago when I was a junior in high school. I tend to try to bring humor in when I'm nervous much like the times during my brain surgeries days. Laughter is the best medicine. As I have mentioned numerous times, La La Land is a place I suppose we go when we don't want to believe reality. This is where I am.

Driving is difficult since I can't get us to the Hospice any faster unless I have a jet but there's not one parked out in the back yard. Despite the seriousness of our circumstance I am focused and am able to stay within the speed limit. We are fortunate that every light is green so far. I am praying that all the lights will remain green because we don't have much more time to spend with Paw before he goes home to eternity with Jesus.

It's after 11 P.M. as we arrive in record time and immediately are at his side. Being curious, I lift the sheet that is draped over his legs to see what this "marbling" of the skin means. His legs actually appear to have this streaking of a pinkish/red color

185

effects that resembles a slab of marble. Originally I had thought that the marbling meant the veins would have marble sized blood clotting. But I was mistaken. Curious Kim is who I am and how I was designed 40 years ago. Dad is still breathing, but appears to be breathing less and less. The nurse tells me his system is shutting down.

All of us are gathered around him and each tells how wonderful a father, mentor and uncle he is and that we love him. This is not news to him because, as a family, we have always been the type to express our feelings of appreciation for each other and I'm glad we did it during his living years.

He isn't able to communicate with us, but we kids still have the ability to recall all the hugs and kisses we received when he was his normal self. This brings me comfort. Steve tells him, "You know I love you, Dad!" Steve's tears are now raining.

Teese, Amy and I tell him, each in our own way, You are the best dad and we love you. We remind him that he has a lot of people waiting to see him in Heaven.

While hugging him I thank him for bringing us up to know Christ and I say, "Paw it's because of that relationship that each of us has in Christ that we will see you in Heaven."

Teese then says, "Hey Dad, we'll follow behind you."

I snuggle closer to him and say in his right ear, "Dad, not right behind, but in a while and it's going to be a great reunion." We all smile. He has always been a man of great humor, too.

He understands me and, as he has said numerous times, "Kim, you are my clone. We're two peas in a pod."

186

Memories of his voice are all I have since he has been silent for awhile now. But his voice is still with me and as my family knows, I like to impersonate people and I have Paw's voice down pat. His is silent; much like I must have been after I was prepped for my two brain surgeries.

I tell Paw about all the family and friends who have come to visit with him over the past few days. I tell him about the ones who are present in his room now. I tell him Dr. Dave and Amanda and our cousin "Little Johnnie" are all here with the rest of us.

During the visit each reminisces and talks about different stories each has about Paw. He always had a great memory; another attribute he and I share. Each has told him how he has made a difference in her or his life and this has touched him because he squeezes my hand and I know he is hearing all of this.

Now, Mom begins stroking his forehead and says, "Clayton, I love you" and kisses his forehead!

It is at this very moment that he actually moves! He opens his handsome blue eyes wide and looks directly into Mom's beautiful green eyes. He wiggles his eyebrows up and down twice as if he's trying to communicate with her. This is totally astounding! It makes me say, "Wow, he's coming out of it!" Quickly though, he lets out a "puff" sound with his lips and closes his eyes. I turn to his nurse and say, "Is that it?"

She says, "Yes, he's taken his final breath. He's gone." I look to my left at the wall clock and the time now is 12:36 a.m. I turn to his nurse and hug her and thank her for having the insight of knowing his life was literally minutes away. I say, "Thank you for this gift of time." I'm blessed that we are here as he passes. I would never trade these last minutes of his life for anything. I'm grateful we had a life time with the love of our earthly father Clayton Manning. He now has an eternity of love with his heavenly Father who created him.

We all hug and are weeping in the loss of our father and our mom's soul mate of 54 plus years of marriage. Little Johnnie is present and is grieving. He has been down a rough road himself with the loss of his father, Paw's brother and our Uncle Johnnie, just recently to cancer. Uncle Alonza, Paw's his last living brother, who lives in North Carolina just happened to come see Paw this past May (6 months ago). What a blessing their daughter my cousin Susie gave him and Aunt Essie. She felt the need to drive to Indiana to finish some spiritual business at her former church of her youth and she asked her parents to come along for the ride. They also got to meet Matt for the first time because he was visiting. No coincidence but another one of God's divine appointments.

Amanda and Dave are weeping and grieving for our loss. All his grandchildren are at home but will miss their wonderful Grandpa Manning, too. I have lots of calls to make. I call and tell Uncle Alonza about Paw's passing and he says, "I'd never trade that time we spent with him back in May for nothing. And you know what? He's in a much better place; Heaven! He's getting to see momma and daddy too."

CHAPTER | 45

A Season for Visitation and a Funeral

So many friends. Clayton Manning was a wonderful, loving husband and our loving, giving, caring earthly father. He has warmly touched many people's lives. We have all lost a great man who loved the Lord with all his being. Heaven has gained a new angel to keep watch over us. He will be missed by many friends, acquaintances, neighbors and co-workers. Those who know him were most definitely touched by this southern gentleman who lived out his faith so boldly. He is unforgettable in every way.

During the visitation, many people come to pay their respects to Paw; included are lots of his and our friends from church and even former neighbors from the eastside where we kids grew up. And more than a dozen co-workers at Western Electric, where he spent 36 working years of his life, are here to show their respect for the friend they nick-named, "Rebel." We all jumped at calling him Rebel and it stuck. Some of us called him "Reb." "I want you to know something; you had a great father and all of us will miss him dearly!" I will cherish these sentiments.

I can say this; he never lost his southern roots or his heavy accent from North Carolina. People would often say, "Where are you from?" And he'd say, "North Carolina." I bet they thought he was just here in Indiana visiting since he sounded as though he'd never left. He loved going to the Mayberry Café in Danville, Indiana. It reminded him of home sweet home North Carolina, especially with the Andy Griffith Show playing on the numerous wall televisions there. He still would say things like, "Ya'll come back now, ya hear," and instead of saying "whatever" he'd say, "ever what" which would always crack my good friend Christi and me up. And when he'd go to his favorite buffet for a late lunch with mom, Amy, Steve and Dr. Dave, he'd strike up conversations with the workers who knew him and with others eating there, too, and some times I'd hear, "How ya'll doing?

I have many good memories. I'm grateful that God has given me so many blessings and one of the many is my memory despite having had two brain surgeries. Remember, I'm the one that has the best memory of all the children in our family and I got that from my Paw. Another "God thing" for sure! I'm blessed beyond measure to still have a good mind.

Getting back to the visitation, once again Rachel uses her God-given talents, words instead of a drawing. These words come straight from her tender heart. She sits at the cherry wood desk behind the family photos displayed in the visitation room and in her best handwriting she pens the words on paper: "Grandpa, there are a lot of people here today who came to see you. That means a lot of people love you. We will miss you a lot but God has prepared a great place for you in Heaven. You are the greatest grandpa. We will see you in Heaven."

After reading it, Tom and I shed heartfelt tears. What a testimony to her young soul and the faith in Christ she has! This Scripture verse comes to mind not only for Tom and me with our children but also for my siblings:

Train a child in the way he should go, and when he is old he will not turn from it.

(Proverbs 22:6)

She walks her poem proudly over to his open casket and places it on his chest so all will know what a wonderful grandpa he is and how his hope is in Heaven and that it is the same as hers. She has the faith and hope that she will see him again. She tells us she wants him to keep her original artwork because, she says, "I made it for him. It's his." The next day and during the funeral it is included in his casket when it is closed and being wheeled to the hurst which will take him to the burial site. It truly is a masterpiece which we will never forget. I'm surely glad that I was able to make a copy of it. Rachel is God's gift to us all.

Think of this: Our life matters to God and each of us has gifts from God.

Our hearts are touched by her tender heart's love for her grandpa and her young faith in The Lord. This hope brings her God's peace.

Dear Readers, is your hope in Heaven? His Word tells us:

Those who hope in the Lord will renew their strength...
(Isaiah 40:31)

I can do everything through Him who gives me strength.
(Philippians 4:13)

He gives strength to the weary and increases the power of the weak.

(Isaiah 40:29)

Be joyful in hope, patient in affliction, faithful in prayer.
(Romans 12:12)

For everything that was written in the past was written to teach us, so that through endurance and the encouragement of the Scriptures we might have hope.

(Romans 15:4)

Our citizenship isn't here on Earth:

But our citizenship is in Heaven...

(Philippians 3:20)

Heaven is a real place:

Do not let your hearts be troubled. Trust in God, trust also in Me. In My house are many rooms; if it were not so, I would have told you. I am going there to prepare a place for you.

(John 14:1-2)

Do you not know? Have you not heard? The Lord is the everlasting God, the Creator of the ends of the earth. He will not grow tired or weary, and His understanding no one can fathom...but those who hope in the Lord will renew their strength. They will soar on wings like eagles...

(Isaiah 40:28 and 31)

My faith is in You, Lord, my hope is in You, Lord my strength is in You, Lord!

192

CHAPTER | 46

Conclusion

At my routinely scheduled MRI today, something continues to be present on the scan. It hasn't grown in the past 24 months since my last surgery so I'm told it could just be scar tissue. This is good news and I continue to give God all the glory. I trust and know God is faithful and He has my life under control. I have an attitude of gratitude and I know that I'm still here on earth for God's intentional purpose. This is until He calls me home as He did my earthly father. My hope is not in this world but in Christ the Lord. Only with that kind of hope will I be able to continue.

Yes, times are sad without my Paw. But I know that one day I will see him again in Heaven. This is the same hope that gets me through the many rough days that lie ahead and the many nights I sit up and ponder life. I know that God has purposed each of us on earth for His divine purpose.

I'm thinking right now that I'm blessed still to be alive and to have witnessed all that has happened; even though at times, it can be extremely sad. Season come and go and I know the reasons for each of these season; spiritual growth.

I'm grateful still to have life and not just a pulse. Paw made a difference in many people's lives. I, too, have the capability to make some kind of a difference in this world: For God's glory! Think about it...we all can and do make differences in someone's life everyday. Is it for God's glory?

Life and death; I pray that if you are searching for peace, joy and hope that you find it. It is in Christ Jesus. God bless ya'll. It's my Paw in me who sowed those Southern oats. Life is precious so treat it thus. The Good Word tells us that we are not promised tomorrow.

So live out your divine intentional purpose, complements of the Creator. You are precious in His sight.

> *I lift my eyes to the hills - where does my help come from?*
> *My help comes from the Lord, the Maker of heaven and*
> *earth.*
>
> (Psalm 121:1-2)

This is my life verse in the good and sad times.

I thought of this last night as my mind was brainstorming for more material for you dear readers:

L - live
I - it
F - for
E - eternity

I have received many cards of hope and encouragement thus far during my journey. I want to share with you this one in particular. I ask that all who may be facing storms take these words to heart:

> "The need you face is great, but the grace that is yours in Christ is even greater. May your heart and your faith stay fixed upon Him as you go through any difficulty! Be assured that He is holding your hand and will not let go!"

His Word promises and assures us. "So do not fear, for I am with you; do not be dismayed, for I am your God. I will strengthen you and help you; I will uphold you with My righteous right hand" (Isaiah 41:10). As I wrote earlier, this is the verse that God literally gave me during my stormy time when I bowed before Him on bended knees.

I make bold to challenge you to spend time with the Lord today. He is at your door knocking; so welcome Him now. He is the one who holds the key, but we are the ones who can willingly let Him in. He is the God of love who doesn't force Himself on us but yet waits at the door for us to open our hearts unto Him. He has given all of us free will so each of us has a choice. If you choose God, you will spend eternity with Him. Eternity with God is in Heaven; without Him and His mercy, it's eternity in Hell.

᠅ "Know Him, know peace, no Him, no peace." I share this from reading it on our friend Mary's bumper sticker. "With firsthand knowledge, I stand firm to let you know this peace is real and does exist in the lowest of valleys! Even at death's door."

> *Here I am! I stand at the door and knock. If anyone hears My voice and opens the door, I will come in and eat with him, and he with Me.*
>
> (Revelation 3:20)

It's a NEW YEAR, Celebrate and live life to the fullest. Make a difference for eternity's sake and bring friends and family with you. It's going to be a glorious reunion. God Bless you all!

Remember L.I.F.E., Live it for eternity!

WHEN I SAY, "I AM A CHRISTIAN"

When I say, "I am a Christian," I'm not shouting,
"I've been saved!" I'm whispering, "I get lost!
That's why I chose this way."

When I say, "I'm a Christian," I don't speak
with human pride, I'm confessing that I stumble -
needing God to be my guide.

When I say, "I'm a Christian," I'm not trying to
be strong, I'm professing that I'm weak
and pray for strength to carry on.

When I say, "I'm a Christian," I'm not bragging
of success. I'm admitting I've failed and
cannot ever pay the debt.

When I say, "I'm a Christian,"
I don't think I know it all, I submit to my
confusion asking humbly to be taught.

When I say, "I'm a Christian,"
I'm not claiming to be perfect, my flaws
are far too visible but God believes I'm worth it.
When I say, "I'm a Christian,"
I still feel the sting of pain. I have my share of
heartache which is why I seek His name.

When I say, "I'm a Christian," I do not wish to judge,
I have no authority - I only know I'm loved

Written by Carol Wimmer Copyright 1988
Used by permission

196

EMERGENCY NUMBERS

Call immediately!

When in sorrow: call John 14
When men fail you: call Psalm 27
When you have sinned: call Psalm 51
When you worry: call Matthew 6:19-34
When you are in danger: call Psalm 91
When God seems far away: call Psalm 139
When your faith needs stirring: call Hebrews 11
When you are lonely and fearful: call Psalm 23
When you grow bitter and critical: call I Corinthians 13
When you feel down and out: call Romans 8:1-30
When you want peace and rest: call Matthew 11:25-30
When the world seems bigger than God: call Psalm 90
When you want Christian assurance: call Roman 8:1-30
When you leave home for labor/ travel: call Psalm 121
When your prayers grow narrow or selfish: call Psalm 67
When you want courage for a task: call Joshua 1
When you think of investments and returns: call Mark 10
If you are depressed: call Psalm 27
If your pocketbook is empty: call Psalm 37
If you are losing confidence in people: call I Corinthians 13
If people seem unkind: call John 15
If discouraged about your work: call Psalm 126
If self pride/greatness takes hold: call Psalm 19
If you want to be fruitful: call John 15
For understanding of Christianity: call 2 Corinthians 5:15-19
For a great invention/opportunity: call Isaiah 55
For how to get along with fellow men: call Romans 12
For Paul's secret to happiness: call Colossians 3:12-17

197

ALTERNATE NUMBERS:

For dealing with fear: call Psalm 34:7
For security: call Psalm 121:3
For assurance: call Mark 8:35
For reassurance: call Psalm 145:18

PLEASE NOTE:

Emergency numbers may be dialed direct.
No operator assistance is necessary.
All lines to Heaven are open 24 hours a day!
Feed your FAITH, and DOUBT will starve to death!

WHEN IN DOUBT TRY...

*The Lord is my Shepherd, **That's Relationship**! I shall not be in want. **That's Supply**! He makes me lie down in green pastures, **That's Rest**! He leads me beside the still waters, **That's Refreshment**! He restores my soul. **That's Healing**! He guides me in paths of righteousness **That's guidance**! For His name's sake. **That's Purpose**! Even though I walk through the valley of the shadow of death, **That's Testing**. I will fear no evil, **That's Protection**! For Thou art with me; **That's Faithfulness**! Your rod and Your staff, they comfort me. **That's Discipline**! You prepare a table before me in the presence of my enemies. **That's Hope**! You anoint my head with oil; **That's Consecration**! My cup overflows. **That's Abundance**! Surely goodness and love will follow me all the days of my life, **That's Blessings**! And I will dwell in the house of the Lord **That's Security**! Forever. **That's Eternity**!*

(Psalm 23:1-6, emphasis mine)

198

Psalm 23:1-6 is a verse that gives me strength in the Lord and I pray will be yours too. We all have valleys to go through and mountain tops to reach. I pray yours will ultimately be Heaven.

I share some of my personal favorite Contemporary Christian songs that have truly blessed me in the these tough times. Third Day is the artist and the song is Mountain of God. Next is Artist BeBo Norman and is appropriately titled I Will Lift My Eyes, Casting Crowns has a song titled I'll Praise You in This Storm, and another one that touches me since the loss of my father is by Artist Mark Harris and titled *Wish You Were Here*. I encourage you to check these songs out for yourselves. I'm positive they will be a blessing to you in more ways than one. I'm sure of it.

DEAR | READERS

I hope this journey has in some way blessed you. And to those who may be in a sad valley, I hope that you will find the same strength, trust and peace and hope that can be found in Christ Jesus.

May the God of hope fill you with all joy and peace as you trust in Him.

(Romans 15:13)

The Lord is good, a refuge in times of trouble. He cares for those who trust in Him...

(Nahum 1:6)

Remember what I shared earlier: Life is precious so treat it as such. L.I.F.E. Live it for eternity.

The author would like to know your comments about her story.

You may reach her at knavon@sbcglobal.net or through her publisher at:

CSNbooks
1975 Janich Ranch Ct., El Cajon, CA., 92019
Toll Free:866-484-6184
www.CSNbooks.com

ACKNOWLEDGEMENTS

Here's to Life...

First and foremost I give all praise and glory to my Lord and Savior Jesus. Without His master plan I wouldn't know just how great He is.

To my loving, supportive and caring husband Tom, our children Calvin (15), Collin (12), Matthew (19), Rachel (10), and Spencer (7), I'm grateful for your love. Bob and Chris Malkemes thank you for sharing our son Matt. We are a blessed family.

I'm indebted to my wonderful OB/GYN, Dr. Hua Meng, for being the cornerstone and foundation by finding this tumor from its inception. I thank my specially assigned nurses at the Coleman Center, Cindy Griggs, RN, and Sylvia Kegley, RN, for stepping out of their line of expertise to help me with the surprising revelation of my brain tumor. I thank all my nurses at the Coleman Center for Women and all who assisted with my care while I was at Indiana University Medical Center and the Indiana Cancer Center.

I'm extremely grateful for the keen eyesight and steady hands and expertise of my superb neurosurgeon Dr. Scott Shapiro and the teamwork of Dr. Jamie Miller and Dr. Robert Sloan. Their expertise in their field isn't coincidental either; it's supremely placed in their genetic makeup.

To Pam McCracken, Dr. Scott Shapiro's right hand and chief office assistant, I'm grateful for guiding me on his schedule for both surgeries. She is such a beautiful person inside and out. She is so caring and always willing to take time and answer detailed questions.

I'm also grateful to my anesthesiologists Dr. Keever and Dr. Rosenfeld they are the best in their field of expertise. I'm grateful that I don't remember a thing while I was under during surgery.

I'm blessed by each of my operating room nurses. I'm grateful that I was able to get to know them in such a short time. Nurse Linda and Nurse Roxanne were the lights that shined during my darkest days. I'm grateful that both were destined to be in my path so we could enjoy together the shining rainbow after the surgery. As they both know, God is the awesome one and as I said He did move those tumors right out of my noggin through the skilled hands of Dr. Shapiro.

I'm grateful to my radiation oncologist-neurologist Dr. Edward Dropcho for providing the best follow-up care of me after both surgeries. I'm thankful for his nurses Carolyn and Corrie and their indispensable knowledge.

To my radiation oncologist brain tumor specialist Dr. Simon Lo, I give my thanks. I'm extremely blessed because of his expert protocol for my radiation therapy. I'm blessed with all my nurses while under his care. Too numerous to name, but I give each my heartfelt gratitude.

I thank Lorie at the Indiana Cancer Center for drawing blood each week while I was on chemotherapy. She is the absolute best, so good she is nicknamed Vampira.

I can't ever put into words how grateful and blessed I am to have been cared for by all my doctors and nurses while treated at Indiana University Medical Center and the Indiana Cancer Center. There are so many!

I thank our families, friends and neighbors (too numerous to mention). We are truly blessed.

With love and gratefulness to God I'm thankful for the love of my parents Clayton and Peggy Manning and my siblings Amy, Steve and Terri (aka:Teese).

To my lifesaver, Jennica McCabe, I'm thankful the golf ball you aimed hit me right where God intended.

To Wendell and Susanne, thank you for the most fantastic tour of Hawaii and for the great memories we share. Your kindness and love are heartfelt by Tom and me. We are grateful.

To my family at CSN Books, I'm grateful for your seeing my vision to completion, with getting my story of His glory into print. God bless you all!

I'm thankful to Poet Carol Wimmer who allowed me to share her infamous poem, When I say, "I am a Christian."

Last but not least our friends Andy Jacobs, Jr. and his lovely wife Kim Hood Jacobs have my gratitude for editing the manuscript from its inception. It was Andy who said, "Kim, stop talking about writing a book and do it. I'll be happy to proof and edit it once you have it finished." Thank God the project is finished.

It's because of the positive and encouraging words from all these people that I have been able to write my story. All these special people are in my life and were most definitely in His plans to be included during the cancerous journey.

L to R: Andy Jacobs, Jr., me, and Tom